DRINKING WITH THE REPUBLICANS

DRINKING

with the

REPUBLICANS

★

THE POLITICALLY INCORRECT HISTORY
OF CONSERVATIVE CONCOCTIONS

★

MARK WILL-WEBER

REGNERY
HISTORY

Some material in this book was adapted from *Mint Juleps with Teddy Roosevelt: The Complete History of Presidential Drinking*. See full edition for complete bibliographical information.

Regnery History™ is a trademark of Salem Communications Holding Corporation; Regnery® is a registered trademark of Salem Communications Holding Corporation

Library of Congress Cataloging-in-Publication Data

Names: Will-Weber, Mark, author.
Title: Drinking with the Republicans : the politically incorrect history of conservative concoctions / Mark Will-Weber.
Description: Washington, DC : Regnery Publishing, 2016.
Identifiers: LCCN 2016019737 | ISBN 9781621574828
Subjects: LCSH: Presidents--Alcohol use--United States--History. | Republican Party (U.S. : 1854-)--Anecdotes. | Presidents--United States--Biography. | Drinking of alcoholic beverages--United States--History. | Drinking behavior--United States--History.
Classification: LCC E176.1 .W6749 2016 | DDC 973.09/9--dc23
LC record available at https://lccn.loc.gov/2016019737

Published in the United States by
Regnery History, an imprint of
Regnery Publishing
A Division of Salem Media Group
300 New Jersey Ave NW
Washington, DC 20001
www.RegneryHistory.com

Manufactured in the United States of America

10 9 8 7 6 5 4 3 2 1

Books are available in quantity for promotional or premium use. For information on discounts and terms, please visit our website: www.Regnery.com.

Book interior design: Jason Sunde

Distributed to the trade by
Perseus Distribution
250 West 57th Street
New York, NY 10107

CONTENTS

★ THE PRESIDENTS ★

INTRODUCTION

WHAT BETTER WAY TO CELEBRATE our rich political history than with a book about U.S. presidents—and alcohol! This book is part history, part cocktail recipe handbook, and all fun.

Author Mark Will-Weber has scoured the archives and historical records for the best stories about White House drinking, which is no small feat since a few of them were teetotalers. And while some stories about drinking can be downright downers, Mark has worked hard to keep it light and frothy in this edition.

Republicans are known as the staid, the conservative, and oftentimes the boring. But this book shows that the GOP presidents let their hair down, so to speak. Find out which ones violated Prohibition (Warren Harding), and which ones got a little tipsy with staffers (Gerald Ford). Read about which Republicans used alcohol to help with foreign relations (Richard Nixon) and which ones used it to ply voters (George Washington).

And for each president, a cocktail recipe is provided so you can follow along at home. Some of the recipes are that president's actual favorite cocktail, and others are contrivances based that president's life or background.

We tried to keep it fun, so go ahead and read about the tippling POTUSes, and mix up a cocktail or two to shake things up. And while moderates may be the scourge of the Republican Party, we recommend that you always drink in moderation.

Alex Novak
Publisher
Regnery History

A NOTE ABOUT THE PARTIES

THIS BOOK is called *Drinking with the Republicans*. But not all of the presidents covered herein were actually Republicans. We didn't want to leave out some of the greatest and best-known early presidents; so, after careful thought, we took liberties and drafted some of those early presidents into the Republican ranks. Included as Republicans for the purposes of this book are George Washington, who was an independent; John Adams, a Federalist; and a quartet of Whigs: William Henry Harrison, John Tyler, Zachary Taylor, and Millard Fillmore. The companion to this edition is called *Drinking with the Democrats*. In that book, we grouped Thomas Jefferson, James Madison, James Monroe, and John Quincy Adams as Democrats. In their day, they were affiliated with the Democrat-Republican Party.

GEORGE

WASHINGTON

★ 1789–1797 ★

"LET YOUR RECREATIONS BE MANFUL NOT SINFUL."

—George Washington

A PRESIDENTIAL
PRECEDENT

GEORGE WASHINGTON, America's most famous general, smoothly made the transition to president. His most famous encounter with alcohol occurred when he put down the Whiskey Rebellion in western Pennsylvania. But that had to do with taxes and federal authority. Washington did not have any objection to the potent potable itself; in fact, several years after the Whiskey Rebellion, coincidentally or not, Washington had a whiskey distillery set up at his Mount Vernon plantation—a venture that proved quite profitable.

Washington, like other general-presidents, had to draw a hard line on soldiers and officers who drank themselves into states of inebriation. In fact, the wise general had to keep his eager men in line when they captured hogsheads of Hessian rum after the famous crossing of the Delaware. But he also was ready to dispense a moderate rum ration— as was standard practice of the day—when his men needed it or when their efforts were worthy of an extra shot.

Not unlike Thomas Jefferson, Washington enjoyed wines and beer more than whiskey (if, in fact, he drank whiskey at all). But he never drank in the Executive Mansion. (John Adams, the second president, was the first leader to actually live in the Executive Mansion.) He did, however, imbibe almost daily when he occupied the President's House on Market Street in Philadelphia during his presidential years and at Mount Vernon, his splendid plantation in Virginia.

THE WHISKEY REBELLION

When the words "Washington" and "whiskey" appear in the same sentence, they are typically in the context of the Whiskey Rebellion (1791–1794). To pay off the national debt (the Patriots had borrowed heavily to finance their war against England), Washington's secretary of the treasury Alexander Hamilton looked to tax whiskey. Farmers on what was then the frontier of western Pennsylvania railed against the tax. The whiskey rebels harassed government revenue agents and threatened to burn the barns and stills of farmers who complied with the 7.5 percent whiskey tax; some even threatened to torch the town of Pittsburgh. But Washington squashed the uprising in the autumn of 1794, deploying some thirteen thousand militiamen to the most troublesome areas.

MOUNT VERNON WHISKEY

Washington had an entrepreneur's taste for distilling whiskey. James Anderson, a Scottish-born farm manager working for Washington, knew how to make whiskey from rye and corn and how to build and run a distillery. He pushed Washington early on to expand his two-still operation to five. In June of 1797, Washington wrote to a friend: "Mr. Anderson has engaged me in a distillery, on a small scale, and is very desirous of encreasing it: assuring me from his own experience in this country and in Europe, that I shall find my account in it."

"Find my account in it" meant, simply, "make some money." The distillery did in fact prove profitable. Most of Washington's whiskey sales occurred close to Mount Vernon. Swaps were common. For example, one of his neighbors paid in crops of corn and rye—in exchange for thirty-plus gallons of whiskey and some flour ground at Washington's gristmill.

In February 1798, Washington wrote to his relative William A. Washington:

> I make no use of Barley in my Distillery (the opera-
> tion of which are just commenced). Rye chiefly, and
> Indian Corn in a certain proportion, compose the
> materials from which the Whiskey is made... It has
> sold in Alexandria (in small quantities from the
> Waggons)....

The formula seemed to be about 60 percent rye, 35 percent corn, and a very meager amount of malted barley. Anderson soon convinced his employer on the merits of expansion. At its zenith, Washington's whiskey operation had five copper stills, a boiler, and dozens of "mash pans."

One can visit George Washington's Distillery and Gristmill, precisely reconstructed on a bucolic creek about three miles south of Mount Vernon. Visitors can take the tour from April through October, and can even sample—and purchase—a batch of rye whiskey made authentically to Mount Vernon's original recipe. The modest profits from the distillery benefit various programs at the historical site. There is, however, a cap on how much whis-key the Mount Vernon distillery makes and sells. As Jim Rees, executive director of Mount Vernon, quipped to a *Wall Street Journal* reporter in 2007: "We have no plans to enter the high stakes liquor business, even though it's tempting, given that the name of George Washington would certainly provide us with a sensa-tional marketing advantage: We could say he was First in War, First in Peace, and First in Smooth Libations." Sampling the product, the *Journal* reporter said it had the amber color of liquor-store whiskey, but that its taste more closely resembled the wallop of a rougher cousin—the elixir we commonly call "moonshine."

MADEIRA MAN

By his own strong will, Washington's certainly steered himself to moderation and control. For example, the general was said to have had a volcanic temper—but he worked diligently to control it. Ronald Chernow, perhaps Washington's greatest biographer, writes that George often drank three glasses of Madeira (a strong wine of close to 20 percent alcohol from the Portuguese islands of the same name) in an evening—not enough to be considered a heavy drinker in his day. He also liked lighter wines, such as champagne.

> We could say he was First in War, First in Peace, and First in Smooth Libations.

Though Washington could be quite reserved with visitors at Mount Vernon, a glass or two helped the master of Mount Vernon arrive at a more congenial disposition. As Robert Hunter Jr., a young Scotsman who visited in 1785, remarked: "The General with a few glasses of champagne got quite merry, and being with intimate friends laughed and talked a good deal. Before strangers, he is generally very reserved and seldom says a word."

Yet Washington did not tolerate alcohol abuse—particularly among soldiers under his command. He did not hesitate to discipline those who got drunk on duty; a "fuddled" soldier might be sentenced to a serious flogging.

THE HESSIAN RUM

General Washington famously led his courageous army across the frigid, ice-chunked waters of the Delaware River en route to his surprise victory at Trenton. Among the many "Washington myths" that have gained traction over the centuries was that the victory was made easier by enemy German soldiers who were celebrating a rum-soaked Christmas Eve.

Truth to be told, there is no historical evidence that the Hessians were handicapped by drink; just utterly ambushed by a large force of Americans during a snow and sleet storm. If the Hessians had been drinking, it probably was in modest amounts, as they still had a rather large supply of rum on hand by the time the Americans arrived.

The rum, however, *did* become a problem when the American troops captured several dozen hogsheads (large barrels typically containing sixty-plus gallons) of the Jamaican "spirits" from the Hessians. When Washington learned of this, he issued orders to prevent his men from sampling their booty, but apparently some of the ragtag patriots had already "warmed up" on the recently liberated libation. Given the abysmal weather conditions and the fact that they'd just been through an eighteenth-century version of a firefight, who could blame them—or stop them? As the historian David Hackett Fischer recorded in his outstanding book *Washington's Crossing*:

> In a word, some of the American victors celebrated their own success by getting gloriously drunk and even more disorderly than usual. John Greenwood (a fifer) remembered a wild scene. The men in his regiment "were much pleased with the brass caps they had taken from the dead hessians." Others began to take them from prisoners. "With brass caps on it was laughable to see how our soldiers would strut—fellows with their elbows out, and some without a collar to their half-a-shirt, no shoes, etc."

All things considered, Washington wisely retreated back across the Delaware, booty, cannons, and Hessian prisoners in tow. But the re-crossing of the frigid river proved even more problematic than the original attack, as Hackett noted: "The rum did not help. More than a few Americans tumbled into the icy Delaware trying to leap aboard the boats."

The general was not against dispensing rum or even whiskey to his troops—far from it. It was common practice for British troops, both land and sea, to have their daily rum rations. And the newly formed American army followed suit when it was able. Washington's requests to Congress for supplies often asked for rum. But the wise leader absolutely wanted to control how much the troops could have and when they could have it.

A GENTLEMAN GENERAL'S DRINK

The father of our country enjoyed his Madeira wine and porter ale. But he also liked to sip champagne, so here's a gentlemanly champagne concoction worthy of this Virginia general.

Champagne Julep
4 oz. champagne
1 oz. bourbon whiskey
1 tsp. superfine sugar
6 mint leaves

Combine 4 mint leaves with the sugar and a few drops of water, and muddle well. Add the bourbon, and stir well. Strain into a collins glass, add ice cubes and the champagne. Garnish with 2 mint leaves, and serve.

In fact, in August 1777, Washington wrote to John Hancock, proclaiming the need for an occasional dram or two for the soldiers in the field. Given the British superiority on the seas, Washington noted how difficult it would be to obtain alcohol from the usual sources:

> In the like manner, since our Imports of Spirit have become so precarious—nay impracticable on account of the Enemy's Fleet, which infests our Whole Coast, I would beg leave to suggest the propriety of erecting public Distilleries in different States. The benefits arising from the moderate use of strong Liquor have been experienced in All Armies, and not to be disputed.

MR. HARE'S PRIZED PORTER

George Washington loved porter—a dark beer—especially Robert Hare's Philadelphia porter. Hare, born in England and the son of a brewer, brought his special skills and recipes with him to America and was already manufacturing the good dark stuff in Philadelphia when the First Continental Congress gathered there in 1774.

In a letter home to his wife, John Adams raved about Mr. Hare's porter, but Washington was equally enthusiastic. They loved it doubly as hostilities with England increased because it meant they no longer had to drink porter imported from London. But long after the Revolution had ended, it was clear that Hare's brew had a loyal following—with Washington close to the front of the line.

On July 4, 1788, Philadelphia put on a celebration called the Grand Federal Procession to honor the ten states that ratified the U.S. Constitution. The three-mile-long parade ended with a feast at Bush Hill (near present-day Spruce and 17th Streets), including a generous supply of alcohol—wine, beer, and Robert Hare's much-vaunted porter. Ten toasts were proposed and, without doubt, honored. Each toast was punctuated with the blast of a cannon.

On July 20, Washington wrote to Clement Biddle of Philadelphia and inquired: "I beg you will send me a gross of Mr. Hairs [sic] best bottled Porter if the price is not enhanced by the copious droughts you took of it at the late Procession." (Could this, by the way, be a humorous jab from General Washington?)

> Ten toasts were proposed and, without doubt, honored. Each toast was punctuated with the blast of a cannon.

Apparently the cost had not dramatically increased, as Washington—in a follow-up message in August—penned: "As the price of Porter according to your Account has not been enhanced and is good in quality, I beg if this letter gets to hand in time, that you would add another gross to the one ordered...." Two years later, Washington's secretary was dashing off requests to Philly middleman Biddle and asked that Mr. Hare put up three gross of his "best Porter in Philadelphia" for Mount Vernon "as the President means to visit that place in the recess of the Congress and it is probable there will be a large demand for Porter at that time."

Although it probably did not match Robert Hare's magic potion, Washington used his own porter recipe at Mount Vernon when the Philadelphia porter was unavailable.

WASHINGTON'S "SMALL" BEER

Long before George Washington became a famous military officer (let alone president of the United States), he knew how to make (or at least instruct his servants to make) a batch of "small" beer homebrew with a low alcohol content. The original notation (dated 1757, when Washington was still in his mid-twenties), is housed today in the New York Public Library and reads:

> Take a large Sifter full of Bran Hops to your Taste—
> Boil these 3 hours. Then strain out 30 Gall. Into a
> Cooler put 3 Gallons Molasses while the Beer is

scalding hot or rather drain the molasses into the Cooler. Strain the Beer on it while boiling hot let this stand til it is little more than Blood warm. Then put in a quart of Yeast if the weather is very cold cover it over with a Blanket. Let it work in the Cooler 24 hours then put it into the Cask. Leave the bung open until it is almost done working—Bottle it that day Week it was Brewed.

There are home-brewing enthusiasts who have the expertise to make Washington's "small" beer by following his recipe virtually to the "t."

ELECTION LUBRICATION

Washington famously chose the high road in politics whenever possible. But he also was not a dolt. He had badly lost an early election for a much-coveted post in Virginia's House of Burgesses. That taught him some valuable lessons for the future—including that it doesn't hurt one's cause to pony up with some free drinks for the voters.

In July 1758, Washington—who was afield on the frontier, leading his troops against the French and the Indians—directed his primary backers to roll out the heavy artillery (i.e., the barrels of booze) in a spirited effort to secure political victory. According to Chernow's biography, Colonel Washington garnered 309 of a possible 397 votes—an impressive tally.

Similarly impressive was the bill for more than thirty gallons of wine, thirteen gallons of beer, forty gallons of rum punch, and a few bottles of brandy and hard cider thrown in for good measure. Given the favorable landslide results, Washington appears to have paid the bill of thirty-nine Virginian pounds (a hefty sum in that day) without complaint.

LAST CALL ....

Washington could, on occasion, display a sense of humor about alcohol and—in that spirit—named several of his favorite fox hounds "Drunkard," "Tippler," and "Tipsy."

Today, Yards Brewery in Philadelphia produces a "George Washington Tavern Porter" that "reflects Washington's admiration of Philadelphia-style porters and closely follows the general's own recipe."

JOHN

ADAMS

★ 1797–1801 ★

"In conformity to the fashion, I drink this morning about a gill of cider. It seems to do me good."

—John Adams

A THINKER AND
A DRINKER

J OHN ADAMS, the second president of the United States,
came from Puritan roots. His father had hoped to steer
him toward the ministry; instead, he became a lawyer,
then a revolutionary, and eventually a politician.

Adams helped Thomas Jefferson formulate the Declaration of Independence and helped bring French military
might to the American cause. He also assisted in negotiat-
ing the Treaty of Paris, which put an end to the hostilities
with King George III and England. As George Washington's vice president, Adams—in typical blunt fashion—
described the job as "the most insignificant office that ever
the invention of man contrived or his imagination con-
ceived."

As president, Adams found the significance he craved. He
was forced to navigate numerous treacherous currents—
such as tight-roping a near war with America's former ally
France over the XYZ Affair and political jousting with rivals
such as Alexander Hamilton and Thomas Jefferson.

Historians delight that Adams was one of the most forthcoming and prodigious recorders of his era: he wrote copious letters (many to his beloved wife Abigail) and diary
entries. Adams could be both wryly humorous and descrip-
tive in his writings, almost all of which pop off the page and
bear the ring of authenticity. The result is that we know a
lot about what John Adams would think—and what John
Adams would drink.

CIDER HOUSE RULES

William Henry Harrison went down in history as the "Hard Cider" candidate, but John Adams could have laid claim to that title years earlier. Adams's insightful writings are laced with references to alcoholic beverages he enjoyed—including rum, whiskey, Madeira, sherry, various other wines, beer (especially porter), and, yes, hard cider. The Massachusetts native attended Harvard at just sixteen and fondly mentioned that cider was a staple of the college breakfast table. "I shall never forget, how refreshing and salubrious we found it, hard as it often was," he wrote.

Being from New England, where apple orchards abounded, Adams became well acquainted with cider at an early age and even had an orchard on his own modest farm in Braintree. His references concerning hard cider typically have a medicinal ring to them; he clearly was not drinking cider each morning in pursuit of a breakfast "buzz." His morning cider boost was a habit he carried well into his latter years, as two typical examples from his diary in the 1790s note:

> Tuesday
>   Cloudy and began to rain; the wind at northeast. The men gone up the hill to rake the barley. In conformity to the fashion, I drink this morning about a gill of cider. It seems to do me good.

> Thursday
>   I continue my practice of drinking a gill of cider in the morning, and find no ill, but some good effects.

We rarely hear of "a gill" these days, but in Adams's era it meant approximately three or four ounces of alcohol. This generous shot of hard cider was meant to serve as an "eye-opener" and to ward off cold, or as a preemptive measure against various other illnesses that plagued colonial America, such as smallpox, cholera, or even malaria.

THE PHILADELPHIA STORY

As a Massachusetts delegate to the First Continental Congress in 1774, Adams offset the bureaucratic boredom and bombast with enthusiastic rounds of drinking. Reading between the lines of his letters and diary entries, one gets the impression that Adams was initially awed by the amounts of food and drink available to him in the City of Brotherly Love but eventually felt overwhelmed and sickened by these lavish feasts.

Writing to Abigail a few weeks after his arrival, Adams declared:

> I shall be killed with kindness in this place. We go to Congress at nine, and there we stay, most earnestly engaged in debates upon the most abstruse mysteries of state, until three in the afternoon; then we adjourn, and go dine with some of the nobles of Pennsylvania at four, and feast upon ten thousand delicacies, and sit drinking Madeira, Claret, and Burgundy, till six or seven and then go home fatigued to death with business, company, and care. Yet I hold out surprisingly.

These gluttonous smorgasbords, supported with generous amounts of imported wines from France and Portugal and Jamaican "spirits" (rum made with molasses from the West Indies), no doubt served as necessary icebreakers. As Adams noted to his wife, the First Continental Congress consisted of "Fifty gentlemen meeting together, all strangers... not acquainted with each other's language, ideas, views, designs. They are, therefore, jealous of each other—fearful, timid, skittish."

Adams may have embellished somewhat regarding the "ten thousand delicacies" of food offerings, but his consistent accounts concerning the amounts of alcohol brim with honesty. The delegates engaged in much of their feasting and imbibing at private homes. There were also intermittent stints at Philadelphia's new three-storied City Tavern (also known as Smith's), conveniently

ADAMS

THE XYZ AFFAIR

Early in the Adams administration, a diplomatic episode erupted between the U.S. and France called the XYZ Affair, named for pseudonyms given to three French diplomats. The incident occurred when the U.S. refused to honor France's demand for payments due to pre-revolutionary France, and led to an undeclared war called the Quasi-War. Negotiations to stave off war ended before they began when French foreign minister Talleyrand demanded bribes from the American diplomats. Things might have gone better had they begun with a round of XYZ Cocktails.

XYZ Cocktail
1 oz. light rum
½ oz. triple sec
1 tbsp. lemon juice

Shake all ingredients with ice, strain into a cocktail glass, and serve.

> I drank Madiera at a great Rate and found no Inconvenience in it.

situated on Second Street, less than two blocks from Carpenter's Hall, where the initial Continental Congress met.

Adams's diary entries from his nearly seven weeks in Philadelphia include several other telling references to the alcoholic libations quaffed by both himself and some of his fellow delegates:

September 4, 1774

Spent the Evening at Mr. Mifflin's with [Richard Henry] Lee and [Benjamin] Harrison from Virginia.... An elegant Supper, and We drank Sentiments [toasts] till 11 O Clock. Lee and Harrison were very high. Lee had dined with Mr. Dickinson, and drank Burgundy the whole Afternoon.

September 22, 1774

Dined with Mister Chew, Chief Justice of the Province, with all the Gentlemen from Virginia.... About Four O Clock We were called down to Dinner.... Wines most excellent and admirable. I drank Madeira at a great Rate and found no Inconvenience in it.

Adams later found the Philadelphia beer similarly excellent and admirable—so much so that he penned home to Abigail:

I drink no Cider, but feast on Philadelphia Beer and Porter. A Gentleman, one Mr. [Robert] Hare, has lately set up in this City a Manufactory of Porter, as good as any that comes from London. I pray we may introduce it into Massachusetts. It agrees with me infinitely better than Punch, Wine, or Cider, or any other Spirituous Liquor.

BOOZING WITH BROADBRIMS

John Adams and a few of the other delegates sometimes referred to the Quakers of Philadelphia as "broadbrims"—a derogatory reference to the wide-brimmed hats the Quaker men wore. The religious Quakers, as a rule, did not approve of drinking toasts, but in his diary Adams relates a funny exception, concerning a toast expressing the fast-fading hope that war with England might still be averted.

> 1774, October 20
> Dined with the whole Congress at the City Tavern... a most elegant Entertainment. A Sentiment [toast] was given, "May the Sword of the Parent never be Stain'd with the Blood of her Children." Two or three broadbrims, over against me at Table—one of em said this is not a Toast, but a Prayer, come let us join in it—and they took their Glasses accordingly.

HIGH-PRICED HOISTING

Once the Revolutionary War was in full swing, prices for food and drink soared. Adams wrote pleadingly to Abigail in May of 1777:

> I would give Three Guineas for a Barrell of your Cyder—not one drop to be had here for gold. And wine is not to be had under Six or Eight Dollars a Gallon and that very bad. I would give a Guinea for a Barrell of your Beer. The small beer here is wretchedly bad. In short, I can get nothing that I can drink, and I believe that I shall be sick from this Cause alone. Rum at forty shillings a Gallon and bad Water, will never do, in this hot Climate in summer where Acid Liquors are necessary against Putrefaction.

British general William Howe captured Philadelphia in late fall, and Adams was forced to flee west to York. Fortunately, he managed to find some decent alcohol to drink in that remote refuge.

RUM AND REVOLUTION

Most high school history books focus on England's tea tax. But it was an earlier tax on molasses (1733) that helped light the tinder of revolution. Molasses was the main ingredient for distilling rum, the drink of choice in the prewar colonies. By the mid-eighteenth century, Massachusetts and Rhode Island contained dozens and dozens of rum distilleries, many participating in the "triangular trade" that sent rum to Africa, where slaves were, in turn, sent to the West Indies. Molasses was then sent from the West Indies to America (as were some slaves), and the process repeated itself for decades.

John Adams readily acknowledged the importance of molasses to Americans in a letter to a friend in 1818: "Wits may laugh at our fondness for molasses, and we ought to all join in the laugh...." Adams wrote. "General Washington, however, always asserted and proved that Virginians loved molasses as well as New England men did. I know not why we should blush to confess, that molasses was an essential ingredient in American independence. Many great events have proceeded from much smaller causes."

ROAD TRIPS

In February 1778, Adams (with son and future president John Quincy Adams in tow) headed to France to join Benjamin Franklin in the diplomatic courting of the French, seeking more support and formal recognition for the new nation in its struggle against the British. Adams and his son crossed the Atlantic in the frigate *Boston*, well fortified with twenty-four guns to fend off ships of the British navy. The ship was also well "fortified" with a rum keg, a cask of Madeira, and a few dozen bottles of port wine, to fend off thirst and boredom during the three-week voyage.

There was no shortage of fantastic wines once the Americans arrived in Paris. Dr. Franklin had access to the Comte de Chaumont's wine cellar, which contained over one thousand bottles. (Adams and Franklin did not mind an occasional brew, either, as noted in an April 8, 1778, diary entry from Paris: "Came home and supped with Dr. Franklin on Cheese and Beer.")

When Adams returned to Europe (again on diplomatic missions) in late 1779, he dined with the French consul and others in Spain, reporting in his diary: "We had every luxury... the wines were Bordeaux, Champagne, Burgundy, Sherry, Alicante, Navarre, and Vin de Cap. The most delicious in the world."

> ...the wines were...
> [t]he most delicious
> in the world.

STOCKING UP

Since war with the British played havoc with their usual sources of rum, the patriots tried to grab it whenever they could. Interestingly, letters of that era often trumpeted the capture of rum supplies from the British or mourned their loss when the opposite occurred. In a letter to a rum supplier on November 21, 1778, Adams shows how he tried to stock up when the opportunity arose and, apparently, could even joke about why the order was two bottles short:

> Sir...yesterday, the Rum was brought here consisting of forty-Eight Bottles. Two I Suppose had been used to wet the Whistle of the Porters. I beg of you to draw upon me the Cost of the Rum which shall be paid immediately.

PRESIDENTIAL KEG PARTY

By the time he ascended to the presidency at sixty-one years old, John Adams was not imbibing with the same vigor that he had when he was a wide-eyed delegate to the First Continental Congress more than two decades prior. But that's not to say the man didn't ever throw a celebration with a little bit of clout.

The president hosted a Fourth of July bash at his home in Philadelphia (the building that was to become the White House was still under construction), and by most accounts it got rather festive.

The overflow crowd devoured massive amounts of cake and guzzled down casks of wine laced with rum. (The wine may have been Madeira, which was commonly "boosted" with rum in the eighteenth century to make a potent libation, typically hovering around 20 percent alcohol.)

LAST CALL

Some of John Adams's earliest ancestors in Massachusetts (dating back to the mid-1600s) were brewers. John's cousin Sam Adams also dabbled in brewing and, of course, has a modern-day craft beer named after him.

Despite his own fairly heavy consumption of alcohol and tobacco in his early years, John Adams lived to an impressive age of ninety, dying on the Fourth of July, 1826. His alleged last words were: "Thomas Jefferson survives!" He was wrong. Adams could not have known that his one-time rival (and late-life friend) had died just hours before him in Virginia.

WILLIAM HENRY

HARRISON

★ MARCH 1841–APRIL 1841 ★

"…BE SO OBLIGING TO SEND ON TO PITTSBURGH
AS SOON AS POSSIBLE A QUARTER CASK OF BEST
MADEIRA WINE, ONE DITTO OF SHERRY AND TEN
GALLONS OF BEST FRENCH BRANDY…"

—William Henry Harrison

"OLD TIP"

WITH A TERM THAT LASTED a mere thirty-two days, William Henry Harrison served the shortest stint of any U.S. president. At sixty-eight years old, "Old Tip" was the oldest chief executive until Ronald Reagan entered the White House just a few days shy of his seventieth birthday.

Harrison's untimely death has been attributed to his exposure to the bone-chilling March weather on his Inauguration Day. Harrison himself deserves much of the blame, since he refused to wear a frock coat, gloves, or even a hat. To make matters worse, his tedious speech lasted the better part of two hours. (And that was even after Daniel Webster edited the bloated text.) Historians chalk up Harrison's demise to pneumonia or pleurisy, but that insidious disease of accomplished men—ego—also played a role. His doctors used both brandy and wine in a futile attempt to cure the fast-fading president. The use of alcohol to treat illness was standard procedure in Harrison's era.

Alcohol failed to save Harrison, but it certainly played a huge role in his election. No other race in the history of American presidential elections featured alcohol so prominently as the rambunctious "Log Cabin and Hard Cider" campaign staged by the fervid backers of the Whig Party candidate. The very roots of the campaign theme came from an attempted slight that was featured in an opposition newspaper, a fact that no doubt made its success all that much sweeter for Harrison's army of supporters.

WHISKEY AND THE FORT WAYNE TREATY

Benjamin Harrison V (a signer of the Declaration of Independence) had hoped that William Henry would study medicine. But upon his father's death, William Henry embarked on a career in the army (serving early on as an aide-de-camp for General "Mad Anthony" Wayne in what was then called the Northwest Territories). Eventually he turned to a career on the battlefield of politics.

The future ninth president of the United States used whiskey to lubricate the signing of a treaty that reaped three million acres of prime farmland. In September 1809, territorial governor William Henry Harrison (he served in that role from 1801 to 1813) gathered chiefs from various tribes to Fort Wayne. Harrison made it clear to the chiefs that no whiskey would be forthcoming until their "marks" of consent were on the treaty. As noted in a journal that recorded the events of September 17:

> The Putawatimies waited on the Governor & requested a little liquor, which was refused. The Governor observed that he was determined to shut up the liquor casks until all business was finished.

In addition to whiskey, Harrison (on behalf of President Madison) was authorized to pay some rather meager amounts of money—one thousand dollars to bigger tribes, such as the Miami, and half that to smaller tribes. (Often these sums were paid in actual goods, instead of coin or paper money.)

The Miami chiefs were more reluctant than others to sign the Treaty of Fort Wayne, but it again appears that alcohol played a pivotal and persuasive role. As the journal recorded on September 26:

> The evening the Governor had the greater part of the Miami at his lodgings and in a conversation of some hours…. A Complimentary answer was returned by

the Head Chief Paccon & they returned about ten
o'clock a little melowed [sic] with Wine.

In truth, "mellowed with wine" seems to be both a quaint and
misleading use of phraseology. "Plied with whiskey" would have
been much closer to the mark. Harrison was familiar with the
whiskey strategy; he had used it before with other tribes for other
land-grabs.

But the Treaty of Fort Wayne did not end Governor Harrison's
problems; in fact, it may have accelerated them. Conspicuous by
his absence, the war chief Tecumseh (and his brother Tenskwa-
tawa—a reformed alcoholic known as "The Prophet") had no
intention of ceding lands that the powerful Shawnee leader
believed belonged to the tribes.

TECUMSEH'S WINE QUIP

Harrison had several tense and unfruitful meetings with the
Shawnee chief in August 1810 in an attempt to get him to accept
the Treaty of Fort Wayne. Blunt and outspoken, Tecumseh
refused to flinch and pointed out the obvious to Harrison—specifically that it would be the warriors such as themselves, and not
President Madison, who would be forced to settle the matter on
the field of battle.

According to some accounts of that era, when Harrison told
Tecumseh that President Madison was highly unlikely to with-
draw the Treaty of Fort Wayne, the chief replied:

> As the great chief is to determine the matter, I hope
> the Great Spirit will put sense enough into his head
> to order you to give up those lands. It is true, he is so
> far off; he may sit in his town and drink his wine,
> while you and I will have to fight it out.

Ironically, it was Tecumseh's defeat that helped smooth the way
for Harrison's ascension to the White House (though it came years

A HOT TODDY FOR HARRISON

President Harrison's thirty-two days in office is the shortest administration in American history. And many attribute his demise to a prolonged exposure to wet and freezing weather during his inauguration without a hat, coat, or gloves. The duration of the exposure was partly his own fault. At 8,445 words, his inauguration speech is the longest in history. Perhaps President Harrison had underlying health issues that led to his death. And perhaps a restorative along the lines of a hot toddy might not have saved him. But it would have certainly warmed him up.

Hot Bourbon Cider

4 oz. apple cider
1 tsp. lemon juice
2 tsp. honey
1 cinnamon stick
2 oz. bourbon

Combine the apple cider, lemon juice, honey, and cinnamon stick in a small saucepan. Bring to a boil over medium-low heat, then reduce heat and simmer for about five minutes. Remove from heat, stir in the bourbon, and serve immediately.

> He may sit in his town and drink his wine, while you and I will have to fight it out.

later). The governor-general repulsed an attack by warriors of Tecumseh's Indian Confederacy at Tippecanoe Creek on November 7, 1811. Harrison was in command during the War of 1812 when the warriors (and their British allies) were routed at the Thames River in Canada (1813).

WHISKEY'S WICKEDNESS

Although Harrison sometimes used whiskey to achieve political or military goals with the region's tribes, he well recognized the mass devastation inflicted by "ardent spirits" on Native American populations and attempted to abolish liquor sales by unscrupulous white traders. Harrison's July 29, 1805, address to the Indiana Territory's General Assembly featured a head-on plea for increased enforcement.

> So destructive has the progress of intemperance been among them that whole villages have been swept away.... And are the natives of North America to experience the same fate with their brethren of the southern continent? It is with you, gentlemen, to divert from these children of nature the ruin that hangs over them.

Harrison had also seen how the abuse of whiskey had an injurious effect on the U.S. Army—not only on the common soldier, but also on the ranks of young officers. Drinking bouts often fueled a rash of arguments and duels between officers in Harrison's day.

A MAN OF MODERATION

Despite the horrors that Harrison had seen whiskey inflict on others, he occasionally imbibed—at least according to one of his most thorough biographers, James Green. In *William Henry Harrison:*

His Life and Times, Green wrote that the general typically had a decanter of whiskey on his sideboard at his home in North Bend, Ohio, and would join guests in a glass or swallow a few medicinal sips when exposed to inclement weather. (Did he neglect this practice on the day of his inauguration?)

As a man of prominence and reputation, Harrison also was expected to entertain. That may explain the sizeable alcohol order he put in to Philadelphia merchants in 1813, requesting if they would "be so obliging to send on to Pittsburgh as soon as possible a quarter cask of best Madeira wine, one ditto of Sherry and ten gallons of best French Brandy.... I wish to have the above articles at Pittsburgh upon my arrival there that I may take them down the river."

LOG CABINS AND HARD CIDER

Despite their similarities (both were military men of note), Andrew Jackson and William Henry Harrison were bitter political rivals. Harrison was active in the Whig Party of what was then called "the West" and unsuccessfully tried to beat Jackson protégé Martin Van Buren in the 1836 presidential race.

But in 1840, the aging Harrison and the Whigs could not be stopped. In one of political history's most clever counter-moves, the Whigs latched onto a Baltimore paper's snide remarks—and eventually rode them all the way to the Executive Mansion. What the anti-Harrison editorial stated was this:

> Give him a barrel of hard cider and a pension of two
> thousand a year and, our word for it, he will sit the
> remainder of his days in a log cabin by a "sea coal"
> fire and study moral philosophy.

The Whigs soon re-drew those images and managed to portray Harrison (despite his wealthy Virginian roots and his stately home in North Bend, Ohio) as the friend of the common man. Harrison supporters "stumped" the country—building makeshift cabins, hoisting jugs of hard cider (and whiskey, as well), and bursting forth with boisterous songs. There were dozens and dozens of songs of the "Log Cabin and Hard Cider" campaign, but this is a fairly typical stanza:

> Let Van from his coolers of silver drink wine
>> And lounge on his cushioned settee
> Our man on a buckeye bench can recline
>> Content with hard cider is he.

The campaign's ditties were designed to show that Harrison was "a man of the people" living the humble life and enjoying its simple joys. Meanwhile, Van Buren was portrayed as a dainty, wine-drinking aristocrat and, therefore, out of touch with the laboring masses. (It did not help Van Buren's cause that the country was mired in an economic mess after the Panic of 1837; some of his enemies mockingly called him "Martin Van Ruin.")

> Our man on a buckeye bench can recline/ Content with hard cider is he.

Harrison addressed some of the bigger rallies, including one numbering in the thousands held on the Tippecanoe battlefield site in May 1840. Harrison, who drank moderately, took a few token pulls of cider to soothe his vocal cords. His followers—many under the influence of the hard cider flowing from dozens of refreshment stations situated around the grounds—cheered him wildly for it.

The Democratic opposition, well aware that the "Hard Cider" message packed a solid punch, attempted to push back by portraying Whig supporters as drunken bumpkins and referring to the general himself as "Old Tip-ler" or "Granny" Harrison. But even though Van Buren was the incumbent, the ticket of Harrison and Vice President John Tyler ("Tippecanoe and Tyler, Too!") easily won the election.

THE DISTILLERY SOLUTION

There is some evidence that Harrison had an investment in a whiskey distillery. If so, that puts him in rather lofty presidential company, with the likes of George Washington and Harrison's political nemesis, Andrew Jackson.

Despite his roots to Virginia's plantation aristocracy, Harrison was not rich. Harrison and his wife, Anna, had ten children, though only four lived long enough to see the general win the Executive Mansion; and any income, from whiskey distilleries or any other enterprise, was probably welcomed. He once lamented in an 1805 letter to President Thomas Jefferson that "my nursery fills up faster than my strongbox."

LAST CALL

Harrison once ordered a beer-making text from a bookseller, so it seems possible that visitors to his North Bend homestead also had an option of drinking homebrew.

In 2005, a company in Indiana put out some high-end bourbon whiskey named for William Henry Harrison. One can only wonder how "Old Tip"—given his mixed emotions concerning whiskey—might have felt about such an honor.

JOHN

TYLER

★ 1841–1845 ★

"I AM LIKE YOURSELF A DE FACTO TEMPERANCE MAN
NEVER DRINKING SPIRITUOUS LIQUORS MYSELF, BUT
MY NUMEROUS VISITORS WOULD SCARCELY AGREE TO
BE PLACED UPON THE SAME LIST…"

—John Tyler

MAN OF THE
SOLID SOUTH

WHEN THE WHIGS SEARCHED FOR a vice-presidential
candidate to join General William Henry Harrison's
ticket, they looked for someone who could solidify
support in the South. John Tyler fit that bill—even if the genteel
and mannered Virginian had little in common with those who
flocked to Harrison's "Log Cabin and Hard Cider" campaign.

With Harrison's sudden death—after just one month in
office—Tyler became America's tenth president and the first
vice president to ascend to the Executive Mansion in this
twist-of-fate fashion. The aristocratic-looking Tyler—about
six feet tall, thin, with an angular face and Roman nose—
took the presidential oath on April 4, 1841. A self-confessed
lover of champagne, if he toasted the moment, it was probably with that bubbly French wine.

Tyler fended off numerous assaults on his presidential powers but was almost immediately expelled from the Whig Party
that had helped elect him. He pushed to annex the Republic
of Texas into the United States and, as a life-long slave-owner,
was perfectly willing to allow slavery to expand there.

Tyler died in 1862, at age seventy-one. Because of his loyalty
to Virginia and the Confederacy, the U.S. government did
not honor his death, making him the only president shunned
in this manner. But Tyler is buried in Richmond's Hollywood Cemetery, the final resting place of numerous heroes
of the Confederacy, including generals J. E. B. Stuart and
James Longstreet and CSA president Jefferson Davis.

CHAMPAGNE: "OUI"
FRENCH CUISINE: "NON"

Despite all the hoopla surrounding the "Log Cabin and Hard Cider" campaign, Tyler—like Harrison's defeated opponent, Martin Van Buren—enjoyed more dignified libations than those made from fermented apple juice or rye. In fact, like Jefferson, Monroe, and Madison before him, Tyler was quite smitten with French wine from the Champagne region.

While still a congressman in 1817, Tyler was invited to dine with President Madison and his wife Dolley. In a letter to his wife Letitia about the event, he spoke glowingly about the hostess and the wine but less so of the food, which he found to be too French and fancy compared to his normal plantation fare.

> I dined on yesterday at the President's. He has invited me three times. Mrs. Madison is certainly a dignified woman, and entertains her company in superb style. In points of intellect, too, she far surpasses the foreign ministers' ladies. I wish the great people here knew something more about cooking. They have adopted the French style, and I cannot relish anything they have for dinner in the eatable way; they have good drink... champagne, etc., etc., of which you know I am very fond, but I would much rather dine at home.... What with their sauces, and their flum-flummeries, the victuals are intolerable.

THE WHISKEY LETTERS

If Tyler drank whiskey at all, one must assume that he did so very rarely. But, as a venerable Virginian of the higher social order, Tyler no doubt liked to have some good sipping whiskey on hand when guests stopped by.

In a letter written from his Virginia plantation, "Sherwood Forest," on February 9, 1858, Tyler makes a request of one Colonel Ware.

I am about to ask a favour of you the granting of which will I trust, give you but slight trouble. I obtained in 1844 through your friendly agency, two barrels of Whiskey of Lt. Richardson. It is due to truth that all my visitors from time to time have drank and sung its praises, and it has been so great a favorite, that it has shared the fate of most other favorites and has been almost consumed by kindness. The last carton is now all that remains of it. Now my Dr. Sir I wish not only to replenish my stock but to procure a supply for an esteemed friend and neighbor, and should therefore like to get 4 barrels of it. Can you do this for me. It was and is called Richardson's Old whiskey and I should like it to be the same veritable stuff.... Perhaps the stock is nearly run out, if so I should be glad to receive two barrels or even one. I am like yourself a de facto temperance man never drinking spirituous liquors myself, but my numerous visitors would scarcely agree to be placed upon the same list....

But even prior to that, in 1832, then congressman Tyler wrote home to beloved daughter Mary. After starting with some mild admonishment—as Mary apparently had recently kicked up her heels on the party circuit—Tyler closes the letter by noting: "Harvest will in the meantime be over; tell John to take good care of the whiskey."

Tyler's reference to "John" is most likely his son. What the future president exactly means by "take good care" of the harvest whiskey is somewhat elusive. Did he mean: "Save some for me!"? Or did he mean that he did not want his son to partake excessively—thereby making sure his son would save some for guests?

HENRY CLAY'S LATE-NIGHT GAMBIT

John Tyler was playing a game of marbles with his boys in Virginia when the stunning news arrived that William Henry

IN HONOR OF THE *PRINCETON*

Here's a tasty cocktail in honor of President Tyler's memorable ride aboard the USS *Princeton* and his lucky escape from the misfire of the "Peacemaker" gun.

Princeton Cocktail

2 oz. gin
1 oz. dry vermouth
1 oz. lime juice

Combine ingredients in a shaker half-filled with ice cubes. Shake well, strain into a cocktail glass, and serve.

Harrison had suddenly died—which meant that Tyler would ascend to the office of the chief executive.

Almost immediately, the senatorial powerbrokers of that era—men like Daniel Webster and Henry Clay—began maneuvering to snip away power from the presidency and add some of it to their own political arsenals. But Tyler immediately made it clear that they could turn in their resignations if they presumed to dictate policy to the new president of the United States.

> Well, Mr. President, what are you for, Kentucky whisky or champagne?

Tyler and Clay, in particular, went head to head on the issue of a national bank. Clay twice introduced legislation for it; Tyler twice vetoed the bill, much to Clay's frustration. In a desperate attempt to get Tyler to come around, John J. Crittenden (Clay's fellow Kentuckian, whiskey-drinker, and the former attorney general) planned a party of Whig powerbrokers and invited the president. But Tyler, sensing an ambush, conjured up some excuse and did not attend.

The evening at Crittenden's had suddenly lost its primary reason for the call to arms, but a few glasses of whiskey (most likely "bourbon," a term coined in the 1850s) soon got the wilder Whigs thinking of an alternative plan. As John Quincy Adams recorded in this classic scene in his diary:

> Robert C. Winthrop told me in the House that, after I came away from Mr. Crittenden's Saturday evening, a regular deputation was sent over to the President's house to constrain him to join the party, to which he had been invited but had sent an excuse. On this deputation were Dawson and Triplett. They went over, roused him, if not from bed, after the house had been closed for the night, obtained access to

him, took him by storm after the Kentucky fashion, led him over to Crittenden's in triumph, where Clay received him at the door with, "Well, Mr. President, what are you for, Kentucky whisky or champagne?" He chose champagne, and entered into the spirit of this frolicsome agony as if it was congenial to his own temper. But all this was as false and hollow as it was blustering and rowdyish.

PEACHY KEEN

In his book *The Recollections of Thirteen Presidents*, John Sergeant Wise relates an amusing story concerning William Peachy's visit to the Executive Mansion during Tyler's term. Peachy, a Virginia lawyer and an old friend of Tyler's, called while the president was awash in paperwork, but the chief executive begged Peachy to return for dinner, which Peachy did. Tyler soon was abashed to learn there was nothing to sup upon except some leftover ham and turnip greens.

Since Virginia hospitality was considered a serious obligation to a man of Tyler's polished background, he squirmed uncomfortably as the server brought in the meager meal. But then Tyler had a bright idea, as Wise records:

> During the meal of ham and turnip greens a happy thought occurred to the President. "I'll tell you what I'll do, Peachy, to atone for this wretched entertainment," said he. "We will send for the keys of the White House cellars, and you shall go there yourself and take your choice." It was no sooner said than done. Peachy knew good wine and loved it dearly. Accompanied by the butler the two were soon rummaging the dust-covered bottles in the Presidential cellars, and, according to Mr. Peachy's account, he never had such a frolic in his life. Smacking his lips, with the memory of that afternoon's entertainment fresh in his mind, he declared that it was the only time in his life when

he had more good liquor than he could drink and not as many people as he wanted to divide with him.

THE SNUB: TYLER'S "SILENT TOAST"

In September 1842, the British diplomat Lord Ashburton was about to depart for home after wrapping up the Webster-Ashburton Treaty, which settled some border disputes between England and the United States. Men of prominence in New York City gathered to give Lord Ashburton a dinner and proper sendoff at the Astor House.

As was standard procedure of the era, a series of celebratory toasts were proposed. But so rapidly had Tyler's popularity plunged that when a toast was offered to the president, it was greeted by a resounding... silence. Even former New York City mayor Philip Hone—certainly far from a "Tyler man"—was appalled at the lack of respect for the presidential office.

A subsequent toast to Queen Victoria was met with rousing applause and acknowledgment—all of which only seemed to add to the absence of respect for the man referred to by his enemies as "acting president" or—even less respectfully—as "His Accidency" or "The Accidental President."

THE *PRINCETON* DISASTER

It may not be an exaggeration to claim that "Wine, Women, and Song" saved President John Tyler's life—at least on one occasion.

On February 28, 1844, the USS *Princeton*—a new, fast-moving warship armed with state-of-the-art cannons (one called "Oregon" and another dubbed "The Peacemaker")—arrived in Alexandria, Virginia. Dozens of Washington, D.C., dignitaries boarded there, including President Tyler, and the *Princeton* sailed off on the picturesque Potomac River. A festive atmosphere (bolstered by food and drinks) dominated the day, and the navy men—including the secretary of the navy, Thomas Gilmer—were eager to punctuate the pleasantries with some celebratory blasts from the ship's great guns.

Two rounds boomed off from the Oregon—much to the delight of the onlookers. But then Gilmer decided that the long-barreled Peacemaker should be brought into the act, intending to fire off a round in the direction of Mount Vernon as a resounding salute to George Washington.

As many of the partygoers gathered on deck to hear the Peacemaker's thundering volley, President Tyler lingered below with his twenty-year-old fiancée, Julia Gardiner. He had been engaged in a round of champagne toasts (including what proved to be an ironic one to the Peacemaker itself) and was about to climb the ladder to go up on deck when he stopped to hear a man sing. The wine, his fetching young lady, and this enthusiastic soloist luckily delayed the stately fifty-four-year-old Virginian. Seconds later, the "Peacemaker" blew up—killing six men, including two cabinet members (Gilmer and Secretary of State Abel Upshur), plus Julia Gardiner's father.

Julia Gardiner fainted upon hearing the tragic news that her father was among the dead. Several months later, she (though thirty years his junior) became Tyler's second wife and bore him seven children. The most prolific president, Tyler had already fathered eight children with his first wife, Letitia, who had died in the Executive Mansion in 1842.

THE GOODBYE BASH

Tyler's foes snidely called him "a man without a party" because the Whigs had essentially disowned him early into his term. Knowing his days in Washington were numbered, Tyler planned a lavish farewell celebration at the Executive Mansion, inviting a troop of his trusted friends. The event featured a great feast washed down with copious amounts of the best wines from the Executive Mansion cellar.

In addition to his aristocratic appearance and tastes, Tyler possessed a good sense of humor, which he sometimes directed at himself—or, when necessary, against his enemies. At his extravagant send-off, Tyler is said to have beamed: "Now they cannot say I am a man without a party!"

LAST CALL

Often in poor health, Tyler died rather suddenly (probably of a stroke) in 1862. As was more or less standard in that era, the president's doctors attempted to treat him with an array of "stimulants"—including mustard plasters, morphine, and, of course, brandy.

ZACHARY

TAYLOR

★ 1849–1850 ★

"STOP YOUR NONSENSE AND DRINK YOUR WHISKEY!"
—Zachary Taylor

OLD ROUGH
AND READY

LIKE JULIUS CAESAR refusing the crown in Shakespeare's play, Zachary Taylor responded with apparent reluctance when word reached him that the Whigs were considering him for their presidential candidate.

In 1846, just two years before he was elected, Taylor wrote: "I shall not interfere with the election... nor shall I be a candidate for the presidency." And during the Mexican-American War, when a Whig messenger visited him in Mexico to breach the subject of his running for the presidency, "Old Rough and Ready" supposedly responded with a scolding quip: "Stop your nonsense and drink your whiskey!" (A great line, if true.) But by February 1847—after winning bitterly fought victories at Monterrey and Buena Vista—Taylor was starting to reconsider. "I will not say I would not serve, if the good people were imprudent enough to elect me," he wrote in a letter. Most scholars and history buffs (and Taylor himself given the chance) would agree that Taylor's battlefield skills eclipsed his political abilities.

Though he was raised in Kentucky, Taylor found whiskey more of a hindrance than an ally in the military. He consumed very little of it during his life but was frequently bothered by others around him, such as fellow officers, who had an unbridled passion for the stuff. But it was perhaps tainted cherries, not alcohol, that killed him, making his term as the twelfth president an incredibly short one.

THE "FIRE WATER" FIRE

Zachary Taylor was president for only eighteen months, but he served as a military commander for more than forty years. And his postings were anything but glamorous: Green Bay, Wisconsin, when it was a small fur-trapping village buffeted by the lake weather elements, and deep in Florida, probably camped in some mosquito- and alligator-infested swamp.

During his army days, Taylor also had a problem with whiskey. It wasn't that he personally drank too much of it—he rarely had a few sips, if that. His problem was keeping it away from his own officers, troops, and the Native American tribes, hostile or friendly, in his near vicinity.

One of Taylor's worst experiences with whiskey occurred when he was commanding at Fort Harrison—a small stockade on the Wabash River in present-day Indiana—during the War of 1812. Some six hundred Indians attacked the fort after setting fire to one of the blockhouses. The fire in the blockhouse ignited a store of liquor, and, as Taylor later recounted, the situation looked beyond bleak:

> ...the fire had unfortunately communicated to a quantity of whiskey and in spite of every exertion we could make use of, in less than a minute it ascended to the roof, and baffled every effort we could make to extinguish it.

But Taylor organized a bucket brigade, and somehow the besieged and vastly outnumbered Americans were able to extinguish the flames—while others held off the attack with poised rifle fire. Taylor had fewer than twenty healthy men and was forced to press the sick and wounded into service. Though the Indians eventually retreated out of firing range, the small garrison had lost some food in the whiskey-accelerated blaze and had just a meager amount of dry corn to eat. But reinforcements arrived the next day, Fort Harrison was saved, and Zachary Taylor added a crucial victory (no thanks to the "fire water") to his military record.

THE WINTER OF OUR DISCONTENT

There are few places on the planet where whiskey might be as appreciated as in frigid Green Bay, Wisconsin, especially in the bitter winter of 1818. But Major Taylor, then in his early thirties and commanding a garrison at Fort Howard, refused to pay inflated prices for whiskey to the local traders. (The price of whiskey, Taylor fumed, "was calculated to benefit the Speculator... and not benefit the Soldier.")

Taylor's stubbornness on the price of whiskey did not play well with his officers and soldiers, and he attempted to court-martial two lieutenants when they bellyached about it and spread ill will among the troops. The charges were later dropped, and the lieutenants escaped court-martial by resigning. As for the soldiers trapped in teeth-chattering Green Bay, more reasonably priced whiskey supplies from the government soon arrived, and Taylor acquiesced to the distribution of their daily gill.

NEW ORLEANS COMES CALLING

Although Taylor was little more than an occasional drinker, he was not against others enjoying a drink or two. Once, while awaiting orders in the Rio Grande town of Matamoros in the early stages of the Mexican-American War, General Taylor got word that delegations from the Louisiana legislature and from New Orleans were arriving to pay their respects and toast his expected success in the upcoming battles. One of Taylor's junior officers, Lieutenant George Gordon Meade (who would later command against Lee on the fields of Gettysburg) had a front-row seat to the resulting festivities. As Meade wrote to his wife Margaret on June 12, 1846:

> The old General received them very courteously and having been warned of their approach, he had a cold collation prepared, at which, through the influence of champagne and other spirited things, many patriotic and complimentary speeches were made.

A MEXICAN-AMERICAN TOAST

After spending forty-one years in the U.S. Army, Taylor achieved the rank of major general and the status of war hero for his exploits in the Mexican-American war. Taylor was soon drafted to run for the presidency due to his extreme popularity. As he was not much more than a ceremonial sipper, his featured cocktail is a nod to his notable successes on the battlefield.

Mexican Coffee
½ oz. tequila
½ oz. Kahlua coffee liqueur
1 cup coffee
1 oz. whipped cream

*Stir the tequila and liquor into the coffee.
Top with whipped cream and serve.*

But, according to Meade, the officers (perhaps without Taylor) earnestly returned the favor to the Louisiana visitors the next day:

> To-day a number of the officers of the army desirous of testifying their sense of the compliment paid them by the Legislature of Louisiana and citizens of New Orleans, got them up a dinner in town, to which all the volunteer officers were invited and you can be assured it was a jolly time. A great quantity of wine was imbibed and an infinite amount of patriotism resulted.

Meade felt compelled to add "To show you I kept sober, I have added these lines after seeing the affair out...." One assumes that the temperate-minded Zachary Taylor also was listed among the sober ranks throughout the visit from his Louisiana well-wishers.

WHEN THE SAINTS COME MARCHING IN

It would be next to impossible to pinpoint a more heady time in General Zachary Taylor's much-vaunted career than the end of the Mexican-American War and his arrival shortly thereafter in New Orleans. He was riding the tailwinds of his tremendous victory over Santa Anna at Buena Vista, and the momentum for his Whig candidacy for president had already begun.

Since some of the most prestigious people in New Orleans had already honored Taylor before the war, one can easily picture the festive swell that greeted him when he arrived at the Mississippi port in December 1847. The city leaders invited the victorious general to a lavish dinner held at the banquet hall in the St. Charles Hotel. Dozens of toasts were proposed, and Taylor was certainly moved. As one observer said:

> The General, evidently affected, rose and made a very neat and pretty speech, which he concluded with the following sentiment: "The Citizens of New Orleans—

Unsurpassed for their Hospitality, Intelligence, and Enterprise."

NEXT TIME ORDER THE CHERRY WINE

More than a few historians have suggested that heavy drinking in colonial times (and well into the nineteenth century) occurred, at least in part, because water supplies were unreliable and could at times cause disease. Food supplies—often not properly refrigerated in an era when an icehouse was considered "high tech"—were similarly suspect.

Taylor is believed to have died after consuming large qualities of iced milk and cherries. Were the milk and/or fruit contaminated? It's possible, though the sixty-five-year-old Taylor had already displayed symptoms of poor health while on a tour to Buffalo, New York, earlier in his term. The official cause of his death is typically listed as "acute gastroenteritis."

> Dozens of toasts were proposed, and Taylor was certainly moved.

LAST CALL

Even though both President Taylor and Vice President Fillmore barely qualified as sippers, neither could resist an inauguration night visit to Carusi's Saloon, located at 11th and C Streets in Washington, D.C. Carusi's was one of the most popular watering holes in the capital in 1849. Neither stayed very long, but the party—predictably—went on without them when they left.

MILLARD

FILLMORE

★ 1850–1853 ★

"I HAVE SELDOM TASTED WINE AND
SELDOM OFFERED IT TO A GUEST."

—Millard Fillmore

ABLE
TO COMPROMISE

THE NAME MILLARD FILLMORE generally comes up only when obscure presidents are discussed. Like John Tyler, Fillmore suddenly found himself in the Executive Mansion after the death of a president (Zachary Taylor, in Fillmore's case). When Fillmore became the thirteenth president, he faced a plethora of problems far more taxing than anything he might have dealt with at the vice-presidential level.

Born in a log cabin in the Finger Lakes region of New York State, Fillmore was one of nine children, and before he was fifteen he was apprenticed to a hard-driving cloth-maker. He later attended the New Hope Academy in New Hope, New York, where he obtained about a half year of formal education and met his first wife, Abigail. By the time he was twenty, Fillmore had clerked for a judge and learned law; perhaps predictably, he eventually found his way into politics.

At a time when most elected officials were drinkers, Fillmore stood out as a man who rarely took a sip. But, known for his ability to compromise, the Whig from New York had no problem forming political alliances with men accustomed to quaff down whiskey—most notably Henry Clay of Kentucky, the silver-tongued Daniel Webster of New Hampshire, and another senator of legendary oratory skills, Stephen Douglas of Illinois. These formidable forces, with President Fillmore's help, pushed through the Missouri Compromise, which delayed the Civil War.

NO DICE FOR VICE

Even as a young man, Millard Fillmore was not a rambler or a gambler and certainly not a whisky drinker. He once attended a New Year's event that featured all sorts of entertainments, but the future president was mostly reluctant to participate in them. As he later wrote:

> There I witnessed for the first time the rude sports in which people engage in a new country; such as wrestling, jumping, hopping, firing at turkeys and raffling for them, and drinking whisky. I was a spectator of the scene; taking no part, except that I raffled once for the turkey... and won it. No persuasion could induce me to raffle again; and that was the beginning and the end of my gambling....

THE TEMPERANCE PLEDGE

As a young man in his twenties, Fillmore took the temperance pledge in East Aurora, New York. Fillmore was already serving as a New York state representative in Albany—a city well known for its revelry—when he embraced the oath. But "taking the pledge" meant no wine, beer, whiskey, rum, or even hard cider—the last almost considered a mythical elixir to Whigs, since the hard cider slogan had helped William Henry Harrison capture the presidency in 1840.

Fillmore held (mostly) steadfast to the temperance line. In his later years, Fillmore was asked to speak to college students in Buffalo, and he emphatically stated to the young men: "I have seldom tasted wine and seldom offered it to a guest."

COMMODORE PERRY'S BROADSIDE OF BOOZE

But President Fillmore had no qualms about offering a frightening array of alcohol to foreigners. When the United States ventured out to make contact with Japan in 1853, Commodore Matthew Perry was deployed for the mission. (The actual Treaty

> ....with more than one hundred gallons of whiskey leading the charge.

of Kanagawa was not decided upon until the following year, on Perry's follow-up mission, when Franklin Pierce was president.) Perry was armed with all sorts of gifts (pistols, muskets, clocks, and John James Audubon's *Birds of America* books, among other items) and a grandly worded letter from Fillmore to the emperor of Japan. But good old alcohol absolutely dominated the list—with more than one hundred gallons of whiskey leading the charge.

The United States was looking to establish ties with the reclusive Japanese empire and to guarantee that its ships could count on being refueled and that its sailors would be taken in and cared for in the event of shipwrecks. Whiskey, apparently, seemed like a logical bargaining chip in these particular pursuits.

KEG ME

Commodore Perry gifted a small keg of fine Madeira wine to Fillmore, who accepted the gift but insisted on paying duty on it—even though he certainly could have avoided doing so. All evidence shows that President Fillmore never partook of the contents or even dispensed this fine, potent wine to guests. It was reportedly auctioned off when Fillmore left the Executive Mansion.

THE COMPANY YOU KEEP

Despite the old adage "Birds of a feather flock together," as a non-drinker Fillmore certainly was the "odd bird" among his most prominent cabinet members. The Fillmore cabinet featured some of the top imbibers of the era, with Secretary of State Daniel Webster in the lead.

The cabinet also included John J. Crittenden of Kentucky (a man known to hoist a glass or two of that state's famous bourbon), Secretary of the Treasury Thomas Corwin, and Secretary of the

A BUFFALO BULL SHOT

After serving in the U.S. House of Representatives, as the comptroller of the state of New York, vice president of the United States, and, ultimately, president of the United States, Fillmore help to found the University of Buffalo and became its first chancellor. The Bull Shot cocktail is a tribute to the school's mascot, the Buffalo Bull.

Bull Shot

1 ½ oz. vodka

1 dash orange juice

4 dashes Tabasco sauce

1 dash pepper

4 oz. beef bouillon

Combine ingredients in a mixing glass and shake well. Strain into a pint glass over ice, garnish with a twist of orange peel, and serve.

Navy William Graham. Graham was notorious for all-male drinking parties at his home on H Street in the capital, of which Ohio senator Benjamin Wade once observed: "the quantity of wine furnished [was as] an important topic as anything."

An interesting aspect of the Fillmore presidency was that the president did not let his coolness toward alcohol stand in the way of his guests. Often the Fillmores entertained twice a week, and some multiple course dinners featured eight to ten kinds of wine.

FILLMORE GETS [SLIGHTLY] "FUDDLED"

If this reads like a headline in the *New York Post*, well, it was most definitely a weird occasion. "Fuddled" in Fillmore's day was slang for "drunk" or "intoxicated"—as in: "I went down to the tavern, and my friends kept buying me rum until I was completely fuddled."

A temperate man if there ever was one in the Executive Mansion, Fillmore did, nevertheless, once admit to being "slightly fuddled" after touring more than a few wine shops in London.

He claimed to be doing little more than moistening his lips with the fine and well-aged vintages, but apparently he did this frequently enough to induce a slight buzz.

Fill more years!

Fill more years!

But—to paraphrase Shakespeare, with great poetic license—that was in another country, and, besides, it took place after Fillmore left office.

MAKING FUN OF FILLMORE

Millard Fillmore, partly because of his name but primarily because of his obscurity, has been an easy target for pranksters with a political bent. For example, in 1985 the Associated Press reported that an organization claiming to be "The Society to

Promote Respect and Recognition of Millard Fillmore" met at a Baltimore waterfront pub under the pretense of toasting the thirteenth president on the 185th anniversary of his birth.

But it soon became apparent that the event was more roast than toast (although the thirty or so members of the group did a lot of that, too), as they boisterously chanted: "Fill more years! Fill more years!" Glasses were filled—and certainly emptied—in this toast/roast. All of which led to more barbs. As one attendee cheerfully pointed out: "What [Fillmore] lacked in charisma he made up for in mediocrity."

Fillmore is saluted in a more serious manner in New York State, usually in towns close to his birthplace (near Moravia, New York), but especially in Buffalo (a city he did much for) by the Millard Fillmore Historical Society and the University of Buffalo.

LAST CALL ....

After his stint in the Executive Mansion, Fillmore toured the country, including several cities in the South. When he arrived in Savannah, Georgia, the mayor and the top citizens wanted to wine and dine the former president. Fillmore ate well, but—as he often did—he politely declined to participate when his gracious hosts broke out bottles of fine champagne to toast him.

ABRAHAM

LINCOLN

★ 1861–1865 ★

"I BELIEVE, IF WE TAKE HABITUAL DRUNKARDS
AS A CLASS, THEIR HEADS AND THEIR HEARTS WILL
BEAR AN ADVANTAGEOUS COMPARISON WITH
THOSE OF ANY OTHER CLASS."

—Abraham Lincoln

A MAN FOR
THE AGES

ABRAHAM LINCOLN, the sixteenth president of the United States, might well be the most enduring leader America has ever produced. Like a runaway train, the Civil War had been coming from a long way off, and the inevitable and devastating smashup happened to occur on Lincoln's watch. Confederate sympathizers would be quick to say that Lincoln's election accelerated what turned out to be a horrific war. The venom against him led to the assassin's fatal shot at Ford's Theatre mere days after General Robert E. Lee's surrender.

From the trials and tragedies of his personal life, through the initial botched battles of the early war, through Shiloh, Antietam, Vicksburg, Gettysburg, and the end game that led to Appomattox, Lincoln endured it all, melancholy and ill-fated. A man of weaker resolve than Lincoln might have easily found reasons to drink—if only to momentarily forget the realities of war or the death of his beloved son Willie in 1862.

Rather than drink, Lincoln told humorous stories as a way to soothe and entertain himself and those around him. Some of the plots and punch lines involved alcohol, though Lincoln very rarely—if ever—touched the stuff himself.

Celebrated by poets like Walt Whitman and Carl Sandburg and, more recently, filmmaker Steven Spielberg, the Lincoln story—both the triumph and the tragedy—never seems to fade. When Lincoln, at age fifty-six, was declared dead on the morning of April 15, 1865, Secretary of War Edwin Stanton sadly pronounced: "Now he belongs to the ages."

TRADING SHOTS WITH "THE LITTLE GIANT"

Lincoln's greatest rival in the political arena was the Illinois judge named Stephen Douglas (nicknamed "The Little Giant"). The two men took part in a series of debates as they battled for a U.S. Senate seat in Illinois in 1858. Although the future of slavery was a cornerstone topic of these debates, the lengthy speeches occasionally drifted into the bombastic banter so typical of jousting politicians.

The topic of alcohol, in fact, was occasionally tossed into the fray. Douglas (known to be partial to whiskey) sometimes called out Lincoln for selling liquor during his days as a storeowner. Lincoln responded by noting that he had quit his side of the counter, but that Douglas was still very much active on the customer's side.

Curiously, Douglas also once taunted Lincoln for not drinking, offering him some whiskey during a debate—or, the Democrat demanded, was Lincoln a member of a temperance society? Lincoln unflinchingly replied: "No, I am not a member of any temperance society; but I am temperate in this: I don't drink anything."

Lincoln generally denied Douglas's attempts to tie him to a life of liquor, but he did once admit to a crowd (which responded with laughter) that he might have worked one winter at "a little still up the hollow."

WAR AND WHISKEY

Although Lincoln did not indulge in any real drinking, as president he was reluctant to embrace the temperance force's strict agenda and tired of fending off its periodic assaults on his time. Lincoln often resorted to his favorite defensive foil on these occasions—his dry sense of humor.

A typical example comes from Lincoln's secretary, John Hay. Hay penned this little gem in his September 29, 1863, diary entry:

Today came to the Executive Mansion an assembly of cold-water men & cold-water women to make a temperance speech at the President & receive a response. They filed into the East Room looking blue & thin in the keen autumnal air, Cooper, my coachman, who [was] about half tight, gazing at them with an air of complacent contempt and mild wonder. Three blue-skinned damsels personated Love, Purity & Fidelity, in Red, White & Blue gowns. A few Invalid soldiers stumped along in the dismal procession. They made a long speech at the President in which they called Intemperance the cause of our defeats. He could not see it as the rebels drink more & worse whiskey than we do. They filed off drearily to a collation of cold water & green apples, & then home to mulligrubs.

SEASICK ASHORE

On June 21, 1864, Lincoln arrived by river steamer at Ulysses S. Grant's headquarters on the James River in Virginia. Grant was preparing for what was to be an exhaustive and costly ten-month siege of Petersburg. Lincoln had just been nominated by the Republicans for a second term and would face the dandified general George B. McClellan, the Democratic nominee, in November.

Although Lincoln had a strong stomach for whatever the dire days of war might put in his path, that strength of stomach apparently did not carry over to extended travel by water. As Admiral Horace Porter noted in his 1897 book *Campaigning with Grant*, the president acknowledged his seasickness to Grant and some of his staff officers. When Grant and company stepped aboard, Lincoln and the general exchanged vigorous handshakes and the battlefield commander inquired after the president's health.

> "Yes, I am in very good health," Mr. Lincoln replied; "but I don't feel very comfortable after my trip last

A STOP AT MCSORLEY'S

Lincoln's famous Cooper Union address was delivered in 1860, a full year before he was inaugurated as sixteenth president of the United States. The Manhattan speech, which addressed the Founders' view on slavery, was a rousing success and launched his national political career. He is said to have celebrated his speech (or, more likely, let others celebrate it) at McSorley's Old Ale House, an East Village tavern still open today. McSorley's only serves two kinds of ale—dark and light. In that spirit, the Cooper Union Black and Tan includes both kinds.

Cooper Union (a.k.a. Black and Tan)

1 pale ale
1 Guinness

Pour the pale ale into a pint glass about halfway. Float the Guinness on top to fill the glass, by pouring it over an upside down bar spoon (or Black and Tan spoon) over the pale ale.

> Try a glass of champagne, Mr. President.

night on the [Chesapeake] bay. It was rough, and I was considerably shaken up. My stomach has not yet recovered from the effects."

An officer of the party now saw that an opportunity had arisen to make this scene the supreme moment of his life, in giving him a chance to soothe the digestive organs of the Chief Magistrate of the nation. He said: "Try a glass of champagne, Mr. President. That is always a certain cure for seasickness."

Mr. Lincoln looked at him for a moment, his face lighting up with a smile, and then remarked: "No, my friend; I have seen too many fellows seasick ashore from drinking that very stuff." This was a knockdown for the officer, and in the laugh at his expense Mr. Lincoln and the general both joined heartily.

LINCOLN'S LIGHT TOUCH

If one had to line up the lightest-drinking presidents, then Lincoln might well lead the list. The times that he drank are so few and so insignificant that they are actually noteworthy. His son Robert Todd Lincoln—when pressed by temperance types concerning his father's alcohol habits—allowed this (as quoted in Jason Emerson's *Giant in the Shadows: The Life of Robert T. Lincoln*):

> I never saw him use spirituous liquors, and I do not think that he ever did so—I have seen him take a taste of wine at his own dinner table in Washington, but only once or twice and I am sure it was no pleasure to him.

The observations of William Osborn Stoddard, an assistant secretary under Lincoln, in his book *Inside the White House in War Times* (1890), seem to more than confirm Lincoln's reluctance to drink.

> There is wine here, and a bottle of champagne has been opened! A glass of it has been put by the President's plate, and he seems to be taking more than a little interest in it. He takes it up and smells of it, and laughs merrily, but he does not drink. There is a story connected with that glass of wine, and after it is told he has more than one of his own to tell in return.

Some men who worked in the war telegraph office also mentioned that President Lincoln once had "small" beer (low alcoholic content brew) brought to them, and that Lincoln joined them in a few sips. But given these examples of the president's "drinking," one would be hard pressed to list Lincoln even as a lightweight.

AN AVALANCHE OF ALCOHOL

Weirdly, the fact that Lincoln was not a drinker did nothing to deter people from sending him gifts of alcohol. As Stoddard documented, there was a room at the Executive Mansion overflowing with gifts of liquor.

> There are loads of champagne... red wines of several kinds; white wine from the Rhine; wines of Spain and Portugal and the islands; whiskey distilled from rye, and from wheat, and from potatoes; choice brandy; Jamaica rum, and Santa Cruz rum; and she [Mary Todd Lincoln] suspects one case containing gin.

When Mrs. Lincoln voiced concern about what was to be done with this embarrassment of liquid riches, Stoddard advised giving it to the military hospitals for medicinal purposes. The Lincolns apparently followed that advice.

WHAT THE "OTHER GUY" DRANK

Just days after Richmond fell to the Union forces in 1865, President Lincoln arrived with a small entourage in the city. They went to Jefferson Davis's home—though the president of the Confederacy had fled the city—and there a house servant still on the premises managed to dig up a bottle, much to the delight of Lincoln's thirsty bodyguard, William H. Crook:

> "Yes, indeed, boss, there is some fine old whiskey in the cellar."
>
> In a few minutes, he produced a long, black bottle. The bottle was passed around. When it came back it was empty. Every one had taken a pull except the President, who never touched anything of the sort.

Jefferson Davis certainly did not limit himself to whiskey, as Union naval commander David Dixon Porter found out (and related in his 1885 book *Incidents and Anecdotes of the Civil War*) upon capturing a British blockade-runner in early 1865 and examining its cargo:

> It looked queer to me to see boxes labeled "His Excellency, Jefferson Davis, President of the Confederate States of America." The packages so labeled contained Bass ale or Cognac brandy, which cost "His Excellency" less than we Yankees had to pay for it. Think of the President drinking imported liquors while his soldiers were living on pop-corn and water!

THE FINAL HOURS

That Lincoln very rarely—if ever—put alcohol to his lips in his latter years is well established. There is some irony, then, in the fact that men drinking alcohol figured very much in the last hours of the doomed president's life. On the night of Lincoln's assassination at Ford's Theatre, Lincoln's substitute bodyguard John

Parker (according to some accounts) ducked next door for a tankard of ale at Peter Taltavull's Star Saloon before the start of the third act of that evening's play, *Our American Cousin*. While Parker enjoyed his ale, John Wilkes Booth entered the bar. As Taltavull testified in the post-assassination trials:

> [Booth] just walked into the bar and asked for some whiskey. I gave him the whiskey; put the bottle on the counter... he called for some water and I gave him some. He put money on the counter and went right out. I saw him go out of the bar alone, as near as I could judge, from eight to ten minutes before I heard the cry that the President was assassinated.

Lincoln's regular bodyguard, Colonel William H. Crook (off duty on the night of the assassination), believed whiskey played a role in the president's death. That—and what Crook saw as Parker's abandonment of his post—certainly helped fix Lincoln's fate.

> Booth had found it necessary to stimulate himself with whiskey in order to reach the proper pitch of fanaticism. Had he found a man at the door of the President's box with a Colt's revolver, his alcohol courage might have evaporated.

LAST CALL

Born in Kentucky, Lincoln spent his early boyhood in a place called Knob Creek. Given his famous sense of humor, the non-drinker Lincoln might be amused that today one can buy a premium brand of bourbon named Knob Creek.

ULYSSES S.

GRANT

★ 1869–1877 ★

"I BELIEVE IT HAS NEVER BEEN MY MISFORTUNE TO BE
PLACED WHERE I LOST MY PRESENCE OF MIND—UNLESS
INDEED IT HAS BEEN WHERE THROWN IN STRANGE
COMPANY, PARTICULARLY OF LADIES."

—Ulysses S. Grant

A RISKY WHISKEY DRINKER

IF YOU WANT TO START A SKIRMISH among Civil War aficionados—be they scholars or buffs—simply announce: "General Grant was often drunk when he commanded..."

Or, conversely, claim: "Grant rarely had more than a few
sips and anything to the contrary was drummed up to tar-
nish the poor man's reputation."

Then step back and watch a clash of two opposing inter-
pretations of history collide with great force.

The truth lies, in all likelihood, somewhere in between.
Grant could go days or weeks—perhaps even months—without an alcoholic episode. But when Grant did drink, he did
not do it well. By some accounts, Grant exhibited low tolerance; he certainly was no match for the rough (and readily available) whiskey of his day. Another general said of
Grant: "A single glass would show on him. His face would
flush at once." Even in his own day, accounts of Grant's
drinking varied widely. Friends, like fellow Civil War general William T. Sherman, insisted that Grant was never the
wild drunk rumors made him out to be. Critics and enemies, like newspaperman Sylvanus Cadwallader, on the
other hand, published grim stories of Grant's supposed
alcoholism.

Born Hiram Ulysses Grant in 1822, the future eighteenth
president of the United States might be better classified as
a "bad drinker" than a "big drinker." But there should be
little debate that he was, upon occasion, drawn to alcohol.

THE CHARACTER ASSASSINS

U. S. Grant had many enemies in the newspaper industry. One was Murat Halstead, an editor with the *Cincinnati Commercial*, who dashed off a letter to Salmon P. Chase, the former Ohio governor and Lincoln's secretary of the treasury. In his letter, Halstead fumed:

> You do once in a while, don't you, say a word to the President, or [Secretary of War Edwin] Stanton, or [Gen. Henry] Halleck, about the conduct of the war? Well, now, for God's sake say that Genl Grant, entrusted with our greatest army is a jackass in the original package.... He is a poor stick sober, and he is most of the time more than half drunk, and much of the time idiotically drunk....

Chase (a non-drinker) and others expressed their trepidations concerning Grant's issues with liquor. But once Grant took Vicksburg on July 4, 1863, Lincoln was increasingly deaf to the general's detractors (whether or not one puts any stock in the supposed Lincoln quip: "Find out Grant's brand of whiskey and send some to my other generals"). And it wasn't long before Lincoln brought Grant to the East and promoted him, with an aim to end the war.

THE MEDICINAL DEFENSE

When Halstead's poisonous letter came to light in 1885, Grant was dead. But General William Tecumseh Sherman, always quick-tempered in Grant's defense, launched a spirited counterattack against the charges, which had been reprinted in the *New York Times*.

New York Times reporter: "The [Halstead] letter states that Grant was drunk at [the Battle of Fort] Donelson and surprised and whipped at Shiloh."

Sherman responded:

That is a pure lie. Gen. Grant never was drunk. At Donelson he won a great victory and at Shiloh we had two hard days' fighting; that doesn't much look like drunkenness, does it? Of course, Gen. Grant took a glass of wine or whisky occasionally. It was necessary. I took a glass of whisky myself once in a while. We could never have resisted the climate otherwise. Sometimes we worked knee-deep in water; at others we were exposed to unusual fatigues. But to assert that there was anything like drunkenness is a shameful untruth.

One must recall that Sherman's comments about Grant come through the filter of a friendship forged in the furnace of war. When Sherman suffered something of a nervous breakdown during the Kentucky campaign early in the war, the newspapers hostile to him (some of the same also venomous to Grant) claimed he was insane. But Grant took Sherman under his wing, and, eventually, one of the most successful Union generals was resurrected.

Late in the war, after Sherman captured Savannah, a journalist tried to get him to compare his attributes to Grant's. Sherman snapped: "General Grant is a great general. I know him well. He stood by me when I was crazy, and I stood by him when he was drunk; and now, sir, we stand by each other always."

LONELY DAZE

But the facts show that Grant was a man long familiar with John Barleycorn. Hamlin Garland wrote a sympathetic Grant biography, but he does trace the man's drinking habits back, most likely, to Grant's stint in the Mexican-American War in his early twenties. A lonely assignment to the Pacific Northwest afterwards, however, was another matter. Most of Grant's biographers trace his problem drinking to that time period. Alone and far from his beloved wife Julia and his growing family, Grant appears to have sought solace in the bottle. He allegedly was inebriated on the day he was to hand

THE "BUTCHER" GENERAL AND THE OLD CROW

Fairly or unfairly, U.S. Grant is remembered for two things: his at-all-costs victories on Civil War battlefields, and his penchant for Old Crow Bourbon Whiskey. Hence, here we present the Bloody Crow. The Bloody Mary is among the most popular and familiar cocktails; this Bloody Crow, concocted with whiskey instead of vodka, takes on a deeper, richer flavor.

Bloody Crow

2 oz. Old Crow Bourbon Whiskey

4 oz. tomato juice

1 tbsp. fresh lime juice

½ tsp. fresh horseradish

2 dashes Worcestershire sauce

2 dashes hot sauce

Salt and pepper

Add the vodka, tomato juice, lime juice, and horseradish to a tall glass filled with ice. Add Worcestershire sauce, hot sauce, salt, and pepper. Stir and serve with one celery stalk and one lime wedge as garnish.

> Find out Grant's
> brand of whiskey
> and send some
> to my other
> generals.

out pay to the enlisted soldiers, and had to resign.

But the all-hands-on-deck crisis of the Civil War rejuvenated Grant's military career. His first appointment was as a colonel in the state militia—hardly a lofty perch—but within two years he was rising rapidly in the Union officer ranks. How did he do it? Grant had, if not flash and brilliance, a gritty stick-to-it-iveness. And that attribute overrode all his flaws in the long run, including whatever sporadic urges he seems to have had for alcohol.

THE VICKSBURG FIX

The Vicksburg campaign was arguably the most precarious tightrope walk of Grant's career. Had he failed, Grant could have plunged into the abyss of relative obscurity, as yet another hapless commander dismissed by Lincoln—but he did not. Grant's capture of the strategic city on the Mississippi River bluff on July 4, 1863, may have happened despite some rumored missteps with alcohol. In Grant's defense, though, these likely occurred (if they did indeed happen) during doldrum periods of the multi-month siege.

Prior to his capture of Vicksburg, Lincoln was not completely sold on Grant's true value. The persistent rumors of unbridled boozing did not help. Lincoln sent down one of his aides—the journalist Charles Dana—under the pretense of reporting on troop strengths. But Grant deduced that Dana was really there to measure his effectiveness and, perhaps, to see if his drinking was a hindrance. Grant welcomed Dana into his inner circle, and Dana wrote a favorable report on Grant for his superiors back in Washington.

Sylvanus Cadwallader, a newspaperman from the *Chicago Times*, claimed to have witnessed the general on a classic two-day bender (including a drunken riverboat frolic, followed by an intoxicated gallop along the Yazoo River) during the Vicksburg campaign. Cadwallader's book *Three Years with Grant* did not appear until the late 1890s, and when it did Grant's most ardent admirers blasted the reports as blatant fabrication. Whatever the truth, Grant stayed on, captured Vicksburg, and won Abe Lincoln's confidence.

An interesting figure in this brouhaha was Lieutenant Colonel John Rawlins, Grant's chief of staff. One of Rawlins's principal functions seemingly was to prevent Grant from obtaining alcohol. The major was only marginally successful at this thankless job and became very indignant if the general escaped for a "frolic." Nevertheless, Rawlins took on this task with the utmost zeal. Even a gift of Kentucky wine from Grant's mother could send Rawlins into a puritanical rant. But Rawlins's true angst cannot be felt in full unless you read his letters. In late 1863, he wrote to his fiancée Mary Emma Hurlbut:

> Matters have changed and the necessity of my presence here made almost absolute, by the free use of intoxicating liquors at Headquarters which last nights [sic] developments showed me had reached to the General commanding. I am the only one here (his wife not being with him) who can stay it in that direction and prevent evil consequences resulting from it. I had hoped but it appeared vainly that his New Orleans experience would prevent him ever again indulging with his worst enemy.

THE NEW ORLEANS SLIP-UP

Rawlins's reference to Grant's "New Orleans experience" seems to confirm an incident involving the general's fall from a horse during a military review held in his honor there in September 1863—several months after his career-changing victory at Vicksburg. When Grant and steed crashed to the ground, the general's leg was trapped underneath. Badly injured, it took him weeks to recover. His enemies believed the accident might have occurred because Grant, after attending a post-parade bash, had been intoxicated and riding an unfamiliar and skittish horse.

The predictable gossip about Grant, once again, rose like puffs of cannon smoke above a battlefield. The rumors essentially followed him until the end of the war.

THE SWING AROUND THE CIRCLE

When Andrew Johnson became president following Lincoln's murder, he soon fell out of favor with factions bent on harsh punishments for the South. In an effort to boost his popularity, Johnson toured the country in what was known as the "Swing around the Circle" in the summer of 1866. To add luster and prestige to the tour, President Johnson persuaded certain Union military heroes—a reluctant Grant, Admiral David Farragut, and the brash young cavalry officer George Armstrong Custer—to accompany him.

There is evidence that Grant fell off the wagon during this tour. Repetitive days of train travel and over-feasting (accompanied by fine wines and brandy, no doubt) probably led to tedium—always a trial for Grant. In addition, Grant's chances of an alcoholic episode typically increased when he was required to be apart from Julia for days at a time.

Sylvanus Cadwallader maintained (years later) that Grant gave into the temptations of liquor during the trip. A delegation from Cleveland met the train in New York State and brought food and lots of alcohol onboard, with the general partaking freely of drink. According to Cadwallader, the result was Grant sprawled out in the back of a railroad car.

Claiming illness, Grant skipped the festivities in Cleveland and proceeded by boat to Detroit and wrote to Julia, allowing that he needed rest. (There was no mention of drinking.) President Johnson also told the crowd in Cleveland that the general's absence was due to illness.

THE DONALDSON DIARIES

Once he became president, Grant was fairly careful not to over-indulge, particularly at official Executive Mansion events. His wine cellar was first-class, and certainly he sipped a glass or two at state dinners, but he was careful before watchful eyes.

Thomas Corwin Donaldson (1843–1898) was a close friend of President Rutherford B. Hayes and something of a mover and a shaker from Columbus, Ohio. Donaldson knew many of the Executive Mansion staffers, too, and put down some insightful comments in a haphazardly kept diary—accounts that have not been widely published in the mainstream media. Donaldson knew one Samuel Taylor Suit (he was called "Colonel" Suit, but in the honorary Kentucky use of that title), a man familiar to President Grant and other prominent Washingtonians. Although Suit was best known for his whiskey production (delivered in his famous little brown jugs), vast fruit orchards around his Maryland homestead also produced magnificent peach, apple, and cherry brandies. Donaldson wrote:

> President Grant seldom spent an evening at home. He went out dining with his friends. Col. S. T. Suit, who knew him well, once told me he used to meet him at a private club room... and that he had a partial side for some fine French brandy in his [Suit's] house. Sometimes he was very partial to it.

EXECUTIVE MANSION WINE

The hardships of war behind him, Grant transitioned quite smoothly into the high life of living in the Executive Mansion. Grant accumulated a splendid array of wines and took a direct interest in them. As Secret Service man William H. Crook remarked:

> General Grant particularly loved to have a few friends for dinner.... He chose the wines himself, and gave directions that they should be served at the proper

temperature...General Grant was an open-handed lavish host. I remember one wine bill which impressed me very much at the time—$1,800 for champagne alone.

Crook also related a wine-related mishap, involving a particularly esteemed vintage.

It was brought out for one of the big dinners, and the President went himself, with Henry and Edgar, two of the servants, to have it drawn off into eight large decanters. On the way down, Henry stumbled and fell, breaking the four decanters he was carrying. The President turned and looked at him, but didn't express his feelings further. When they got downstairs General Grant said to Beckley, the steward:

"Get four other decanters and go to the garret and fill them, but don't let Henry go again!"

Although Grant was known for treating his staff well, the unlucky servant admitted that the president's disapproving stare had made him wish he could "go through the floor."

LAST CALL

The biggest scandal during Grant's presidency was called the Whiskey Ring—a conspiracy in the mid-1870s that allowed the perpetrators to skim millions of uncollected tax dollars that should have come from liquor production. Although most historians agree Grant had no direct knowledge of the massive fraud, some of his closest associates were prosecuted for their involvement.

HAYES

★ 1877–1881 ★

"MUST SWEAR OFF FROM SWEARING. BAD HABIT."
—Rutherford B. Hayes

THE TEETOTALER AND
THE SINGLE VOTE

RUTHERFORD B. HAYES—a Civil War hero who went on to become a U.S. congressman, governor of Ohio, and then the nineteenth president of the United States—did not exactly "sweep" into the Executive Mansion. In fact, his Democratic opponent, the squeaky-voiced Samuel J. Tilden of New York, tabulated more votes. The Compromise of 1877 (a deal in which Southern factions consented to support the Republican Hayes if he would agree to remove Union troops from the South) allowed Hayes to prevail by a single electoral vote. But Hayes's administration suffered much from congressional backlash, both from defeat-bitter Democrats and Republican radicals who were not yet prepared to pardon the South.

After such a hotly contested campaign and tumultuous beginning, a round of good stiff drinks might have been in order. But the Hayes Executive Mansion left behind a rather different social legacy. Never a big drinker, Hayes had been known to have an occasional beer in his younger days in Cincinnati's "Over-the-Rhine" German section. However, most likely driven by his wife's wishes (Lucy was a committed teetotaler), the president appeared to embrace a ban on alcohol at Executive Mansion functions.

As John Sergeant Wise remarked: "With all her lovable and excellent traits, Mrs. Hayes was more or less a crank on this subject... President Hayes admired and respected Mrs. Hayes greatly and deferred to her demands about liquor, but I do not think he was himself in the least fanatical on the subject."

THE DAYS OF WINE AND RUSSIANS

Just weeks after President Hayes and his wife moved into the Executive Mansion, the residence was abuzz. The Russians were coming—specifically Alexis and Constantine, the young adult sons of Czar Alexander II. This event was incredibly exciting, but it also created a dilemma: what to offer their esteemed and somewhat exotic guests in way of a thirst-quencher? It was well known that the first lady had pledged not to serve intoxicating beverages in the Executive Mansion.

After much hand-wringing and temple-massaging, it was decided that wine should—and would—be offered. Secretary of State William Evarts took the heat on this incident, insisting that America would look uncultured if its leaders did not offer the Eastern Europeans what they were accustomed to drinking at an extravagant dinner. The young grand dukes from Russia, perhaps oblivious to all the fuss, arrived and drank their wine along with all the trimmings of a state feast. Predictably, President Hayes and the first lady did not imbibe. In the aftermath, temperance forces, which had lent support to Hayes in the recent election, protested that any wine, for any reason, had been served.

THE SIDEBOARD AND THE SALOON

As presidential artifacts go, the "Lucy Hayes Sideboard" is arguably one of the most noteworthy—at least to aficionados of White House decorative history. The sideboard is a valuable piece of art: rich mahogany, ornately carved by one of the most celebrated woodworkers of nineteenth-century America, Henry Fry of Cincinnati. The piece was ordered while Hayes was president and stood in the Executive Mansion dining room along with an accompanying carving table, also made by Fry and his associates. Since the Hayes Executive Mansion was renowned for not serving alcoholic beverages, the only liquids to appear on the table were tea, coffee, water, punch, and lemonade. (Lucy Hayes was aptly nicknamed "Lemonade Lucy" by historians.) Visiting journalists and dignitaries, among others, found this condition especially bleak, and most likely the beauty of Fry's mahogany masterpiece was lost upon those members of the fourth estate.

> Mrs. Hayes was more or less a crank on this subject.

The sideboard still loomed majestically in the dining room when the Hayes family left the Executive Mansion after one term. James Garfield moved in, but, due to an assassin's bullet, his service proved quite brief. When Chester A. Arthur—a polished New Yorker with extravagant tastes—took over the leadership reins, he opted for renovations at the Executive Mansion. In the midst of this zealous makeover, wagonloads of furniture and other items were unceremoniously dumped into the hands of a secondhand junk dealer. The Lucy Hayes Sideboard ended up as part of this hapless haul. The secondhand junk dealer promptly sold (for a mere eighty-five dollars) the Lucy Hayes Sideboard, ironically, to John M. Frank, owner of a Washington brewery and beer garden.

Stirring up even more of a brouhaha, a rumor persisted that the sideboard had been a gift from the Women's Christian Temperance Union, in recognition of Lucy's pledge to keep Executive Mansion events sans alcohol. But the facts suggest that an Executive Mansion official ordered the sideboard at the Hayeses' request. Nevertheless, this notion of the Lucy Hayes Sideboard being a gift from the WCTU is still printed (and presented as fact) today.

A *New York Times* article on February 28, 1903, quoted John Wesley Gaines, a Democrat from Tennessee, voicing his outrage to his fellow House representatives: "It is a fact," said Mr. Gaines, "that the mahogany sideboard given to Mrs. Hayes while she was in the White House is down here in a Washington brewery. I saw it there yesterday."

HAYES AND THE LORDS AND LADIES

President Hayes is the most famous alumnus of Kenyon College in Gambier, Ohio. As the college was bankrolled by English Lords Kenyon and Gambier, the college took on the nickname of Lords. When Kenyon accepted women in 1969, they became the Lords and Ladies. In honor of Hayes's collegiate days, here is the Lord and Lady Cocktail.

Lord and Lady Cocktail

1 ½ oz. dark rum
½ oz. coffee liqueur

Pour the rum and coffee liqueur into an old-fashioned glass almost filled with ice cubes. Stir well and serve.

Although it appears Gaines was wrong about the sideboard being a gift from the WCTU or anyone else, he was correct that it was in the hands of the beer garden proprietor. If the sideboard had supported no alcohol during its Executive Mansion era, Frank was making up for lost time; when Gaines viewed the piece it was decorated with various liquor bottles and "a row of fine old German beer steins."

Webb Hayes (one of the former president's sons) offered to buy it from him for hundreds of dollars. But Mr. Frank, apparently, did not want to part with the sideboard for such a modest sum; he was demanding three thousand dollars.

It was more than six decades later, in 1967, that the Rutherford B. Hayes Presidential Center, Inc., was able to purchase the Lucy Hayes Sideboard from Frank's descendants—for a price of $2,500. Visitors to Spiegel Grove—the Hayeses' homestead and museum in Fremont, Ohio—can view the handcrafted mahogany sideboard that caused so much controversy as part of their tour.

PUNCH AND COUNTER-PUNCH

James G. Blaine, the speaker of the House, felt the pain of thirsty visitors to the Executive Mansion. He once arrived rather late in the evening at the Danish Embassy, placed his hands on the shoulders of the ambassador, and—paraphrasing Shakespeare's Richard the III—proclaimed: "My kingdom for a glass of whiskey; I have just dined at the White House." (Similarly, Secretary of State William Evarts wisecracked that at Executive Mansion events "the water flows like wine....")

Newspapermen of that day—most of whom were known to hoist a glass or two on a regular basis—would certainly have concurred with Blaine and Evarts. Visits to the Executive Mansion in the Hayes term were considered tough duty. There was a rumor that some of the Executive Mansion staff—taking pity upon the dignitaries, scribblers, and other visiting imbibers at official dinners—soaked the oranges in the supposed non-alcoholic punch with some highly potent rum. The journalists and a few other visitors in on this liquid stealth referred to the spiked punch bowl as "the Life-Saving Station." (Evidence indicated that some of the frozen orange slices served to guests also might have been rum-fortified.)

But perhaps it wasn't President Hayes and Lemonade Lucy who were fooled. In his diary, former President Hayes staunchly insisted:

> My kingdom for a glass of whiskey; I have just dined at the White House.

> The joke of the Roman punch oranges was not on us but on the drinking people. My orders were to flavor them rather strongly with the same flavor that is found in Jamaica rum.... This took! This certainly was the case after the facts alluded to reached our ears. It was refreshing to hear "the drinkers" say with a smack of the lips, "would they were hot!"

THE HIDDEN BOTTLE

Thomas Donaldson—a fellow Ohioan, Civil War veteran, and personal friend and ally of President and Lucy Hayes—kept some insightful notes during Hayes's (and later Garfield's) Executive Mansion years. Donaldson often stopped by to visit; he was on friendly terms with most of the Executive Mansion staff and was privy to their observations and jokes. Some of those pranks (as with the allegedly doctored punch bowl) inevitably revolved around the no-alcohol policy. On June 26, 1880, Donaldson noted:

> Now for a bit of future fun about the north doorway cut from the window into the conservatory at the White House. Before the window jamb was put up, Mr. [Edison S.] Dinsmore, one of the White House [police] officials, got an empty champagne bottle and marked upon the label that it was of the administration of President Hayes, with the date, and put it in the face

of the wall. It was closed up by the contractor, and when opened in time to come, there should be fun.

Is it possible that Dinsmore's champagne bottle still resides in the White House wall to this day?

LAST CALL

Hayes's parents once established a whiskey distillery on their farm just north of Columbus, Ohio, in an effort to generate extra income.

As a young lawyer, Hayes belonged to the Cincinnati Literary Club, which served oysters chased with "liberal amounts of Catawba wine," but he also belonged to the Sons of Temperance.

During his presidency, Hayes wished to remove some twenty U.S. diplomats serving abroad whom he strongly suspected of chronic drunkenness.

JAMES

GARFIELD

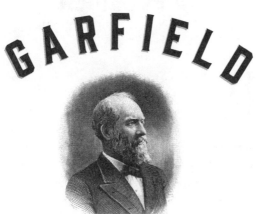

★

MARCH 1881–SEPTEMBER 1881

★

"I HAVE HAD MANY TROUBLES,
BUT THE WORST OF THEM NEVER CAME."

—James Garfield

TWO HUNDRED DAYS
AS PRESIDENT

JAMES GARFIELD was a Civil War officer who fought at Shiloh and Chickamauga and led his Union troops to victory against superior odds at the lesser-known battle of Middle Creek early in 1862. Prior to the war, Garfield had been an academic on the fast track, but catapulted by his battlefield success he won a congressional seat for Ohio in 1863.

Though Garfield was a skilled orator, it was a surprise when he was selected as the Republican candidate for president in 1880. This happened after the "Stalwart" faction and the "Half-Breeds" became mired in a stalemate. Garfield often claimed he never had the "fever" to be president. He went on to defeat General Winfield Scott Hancock, the Democratic candidate—by a mere ten thousand votes. He was president for just two hundred days, and for eighty of those he was incapacitated. Only William Henry Harrison was president for a shorter time period.

Garfield is one of a select group of presidents who were assassinated while in office. A deranged man named Charles Guiteau believed that Garfield had thwarted his ambitions to be named U.S. ambassador to France. The bitter man gunned down Garfield at a railroad station on July 2, 1881. Eighty days later the president died from septic complications.

Garfield was a moderate drinker—he liked an occasional beer—but his doctors, according to the thinking of the time, used brandy and whiskey (referred to as "stimulants") in his treatment after being shot.

ROUGH START

James Garfield was the last American president born in a log cabin. His father, Abram Garfield, was a large-sized character, both in actual size and in legendary deeds. For example, Abram was said to have been a champion wrestler in his region and also a man who (according to one biographer) could drain a sizeable container of whiskey—"and no man dared call him coward."

James was educated at Western Reserve (in present-day Cleveland) and Williams College in Massachusetts. There were no reports of feats involving whiskey kegs, but Garfield did once receive criticism for having a keg of ale on campus—though he claimed to have purchased it for medicinal purposes.

BEER BREAK

As if following the example of his fellow Ohioan—the temperance-minded Rutherford B. Hayes—Garfield neither drank nor served wine in the Executive Mansion. Ulysses S. Grant had left behind a rather substantial wine cellar, but Garfield's time in the Executive Mansion was so short (barely six months) that there were no receptions there that would have required the serving of quality wines or liquors.

According to the diary of Thomas Donaldson, Garfield did venture out for an occasional beer. Donaldson (a fellow Ohioan who had great access to the Executive Mansion under both Hayes and Garfield) noted this in his writings after some casual chats with Executive Mansion staff.

> *Washington, D.C., [Wednesday] Jan. 19th, 1881.*—[Alphonso T.] Donn, [William D.] Allen and other door-keepers [and ushers] at the White House often speak to me of the habits of the several Presidents they have served under. General Grant was generally out at night, out visiting and with cronies. President Hayes usually walked out in clear and fine weather, and always walked home when out in the evening.... Mr. Lincoln drank nothing. Mr. Johnson drank a good

deal and not much wine. General Grant [drank] some, and Mr. Hayes nothing. Mr. Garfield liked to walk out and liked beer and drank but little else.

DODGING THE DRINKING DART

A common political tactic of that era was to accuse your opponent of heavy drinking. Garfield—who, by examining all the evidence, was at most a moderate imbiber—nonetheless had to deal with that political dart during a first defense of his Ohio congressional seat.

In the words of Garfield biographer Allan Peskin:

> There were also some potentially damaging rumors circulating through the district to the effect that Garfield had become a drunkard in the army and was now leading a life of the grossest profligacy in Washington. Garfield was perplexed as to how these charges could be answered. He admitted privately that his life was not spotless: "I have played cards as an amusement with a friend and I have sometimes tasted wine...."

Garfield managed to get reelected, despite the alcohol-related aspersions—and despite his criticism of President Lincoln, whom he saw as too moderate and plodding on the slavery issue.

BOOZE VERSUS BULLET WOUNDS

As was fairly common practice at the time, the doctors trying to save Garfield's life used alcohol (brandy, rum, claret, and whiskey all were called upon) as part of his medical treatment.

None of this, of course, served to save the president's life. With the huge advantage of hindsight—and the advancement of medical know-how—biographers, historians, and modern medical experts suggest that Garfield might have survived his initial wounds had his doctors not infected him by poking their

A CRAZY SHOT

Just a few months into his term, Garfield was shot at the train station about to depart for his summer vacation on the Jersey shore. The assassin, Charles Guiteau, was a fellow Republican with a history of mental instability. Despite his clear lack of qualifications, Guiteau was unhappy with Garfield for rebuffing his request for a plum administration post and intended to exact his revenge. After borrowing fifteen dollars, he purchased a revolver and shot Garfield on July 2. While Garfield survived the initial shooting, he succumbed to infection eleven weeks later. The Revolver cocktail is a fitting homage to this historical incident.

The Revolver
2 oz. Bourbon
¼ oz. coffee liqueur
2 dashes orange bitters

Add all the ingredients to a mixing glass and fill with ice. Stir until well chilled and strain into a chilled cocktail glass. Garnish with a wide strip of orange peel and serve.

unsanitary hands and medical utensils inside the patient in an attempt to find the bullet.

PRAYER, BLISS, AND WHISKEY

Garfield did, for brief stints, seem to gain strength during his ordeal, only to fail again. One of Garfield's doctors—D. W. Bliss (whose given first name was actually "Doctor")—allegedly fielded a suggestion from a newspaper reporter that some people believed the wounded president's health had slowly rebounded due to the power of prayer.

Bliss supposedly replied, "They may think so. In my opinion it was whiskey." And the whiskey used in Garfield's treatment most likely came from Thomas Donaldson's very best stock. In his diary entries, entered in late August, Donaldson optimistically penned:

> No person was ever known to die while using this whiskey.

I told them at the White House that there were two reasons why Garfield would not die: first, He is an Ohio man, and none die in office; [and] second, I supplied the whiskey used, 25 years old, and no person was ever known to die while using this whiskey.

Unfortunately, neither prayer nor well-aged whiskey (nor being from the Buckeye State) could save Garfield. He died several weeks later—on September 19—at the New Jersey seashore.

PLEA FOR PORT

One of the last letters of correspondence between Garfield and his wife Crete (dated June 30, 1881) contained a plea from Crete that the president should bring some port to their vacation spot on the New Jersey shore.

My Darling:

For two nights I have taken a glass of port wine and conclude that it is one reason that I have slept better, but I have only a little more wine and if you can bring me a little more that you can trust as pure port, I think it may be of advantage to me....

Two days later, while waiting to board a train to New Jersey, the president was shot by his deluded assassin at the Washington, D.C., train station.

PRE-REVEREND BURCHARD

Although Reverend Samuel Burchard's infamous political faux pas of "Rum, Romanism, and Rebellion" inadvertently helped elect Grover Cleveland in 1884, then U.S. congressman James Garfield had expressed similar sentiments years earlier. Fearing that the Republicans supporting Hayes had lost the 1876 election to Tilden, he wrote in a private letter to his friend Corydon Fuller on November 9, 1876:

It is very hard to go on with the work of the great campaign with so much grief in my heart... I spoke almost every day till the election; but it now appears that we are defeated by the combined power of rebellion, Catholicism and whiskey, a trinity very hard to conquer.

The Hayes forces, of course, later prevailed in the electoral vote—with a controversial swing of twenty unresolved votes in Florida, Louisiana, South Carolina, and Oregon coming in for the GOP. But, judging from Garfield's letter, even he thought that the Republicans had lost until those much-contested votes helped Hayes take the Executive Mansion.

LAST CALL ....

Temperance forces hoped to persuade Garfield to follow the lead of the Hayes Executive Mansion—that is, to ban alcohol from presidential dinners and celebrations. Garfield managed to sidestep their advances and—at the urging of his secretary of state, James Blaine—he intended to bring up some of the fine wines (left over from President Grant's day) from the Executive Mansion cellar. But Garfield died before he had much chance to sample or share those vintages.

CHESTER

ARTHUR

★ 1881–1885 ★

"MADAM, I MAY BE THE PRESIDENT OF THE UNITED STATES, BUT WHAT I DO WITH MY PRIVATE LIFE IS MY OWN DAMNED BUSINESS!"

—Chester Arthur

THE GENTLEMAN BOSS

A PRODUCT OF THE GILDED AGE, Chester Arthur spent lavishly on fine clothing, rich food, and top-quality liquor. As Arthur's wife, Ellen Herndon, had died suddenly in 1880 prior to his election, his sister, Mrs. Mary McElroy, served as his first lady and partner in crime in extravagance.

Since Arthur's rise to chief executive came about only after Garfield's assassination, few harbored any great expectations for his term. Some contemporaries could not help but register their disbelief, declaring: "Chet Arthur president of the United States... Good God!" His critics maintained that Arthur's passion for entertaining far outstripped any of his political achievements.

Arthur kept a low profile while Garfield hovered near death at the New Jersey seaside. Congressman John Wise found Arthur holed up in his Manhattan townhouse and described the lodging as "a bachelor establishment, free and easy, with lots of tobacco smoke and decanters...."

Nicknamed "The Gentleman Boss," the former New York pol never disavowed his connection to the Tammany machine. But once in the Executive Mansion, he made it clear that he'd be his own man. He was not chosen by his party to run for a second term, and, despite the rejection he felt, it may have been just as well: Arthur's health was already in rapid decline due to Bright's disease (which included kidney failure), and he would not have lived through a second term.

THE WISE PORTRAIT

In *Recollections of Thirteen Presidents* (published in 1909), Congressman Wise wrote of Arthur, the mutton-chopped twenty-first president:

> He loved good company, and his high-ball, and his glass of champagne...

> Arthur was a high liver. He was not by any means a drunkard, but he was a typical New York man-about-town, and showed it in his fat and ruddiness. He ate and drank too much, and died young from the effects of over-indulgence. He loved good company, and his high-ball, and his glass of champagne, and his late supper with a large cold bottle and a small hot bird.

THE INSIDE "SOAP"

Garfield and Arthur formed something of an uneasy alliance—a classic "marriage" of political convenience that helped the Republicans win the 1880 election. They hardly knew each other prior to the Republican convention, and each man was somewhat wary of the other even after they won. Arthur, after all, was the Tammany Hall man, and everyone in the political sphere assumed that he would represent the interests of Roscoe Conkling, his Gotham-based boss.

As the Republicans prepared to take control of the Executive Mansion, they held some celebratory dinners. One such dinner—specifically to honor Stephen Dorsey, the national committee secretary who had helped deliver Indiana to the GOP—took place at Delmonico's in New York City in early 1881. This upscale restaurant-watering hole was familiar terrain for Vice President—elect Arthur, so he must have felt quite comfortable as he arose to address the completely partisan crowd, peppered with a few journalists.

Still flushed with victory and, by most accounts, flushed with a bit too much alcohol, Chet Arthur began to dance dangerously close to the truth about what it takes to win elections. Specifically, Arthur could not help but "crow" about how the Republicans had managed to flip the state of Indiana into the righteous column of Garfield-Arthur.

Some in the crowd (equally inspired by liquid refreshment) began to playfully bellow out "Soap! Soap!" as the key ingredient in the Indiana win. In Arthur's day, "soap" was essentially a code word for spreading around money and other enticements in exchange for votes. But as a veteran product of the Tammany Hall machine, Arthur stopped just short of providing any truly incriminating details; he had not been so tipsy that he did not notice some reporters at the gathering, scribbling down notes.

THE TEMPERANCE ATTACK

James Garfield was hardly buried when temperance forces began pressing their attack on Arthur. What exactly did they want? Surely Arthur—perhaps bewildered by the mere existence of abstainers—must have asked himself that question.

For starters, they wanted Arthur to continue the Rutherford B. Hayes/Lucy Hayes policy of banning wine and other alcoholic beverages in the Executive Mansion. They also wanted Arthur to hang a large portrait of Lucy Hayes, their heroine, in the Executive Residence.

Arthur wanted neither a ban nor a painting. But the temperance forces wouldn't take "no" for an answer. Finally (one can picture Arthur's already ruddy complexion coloring to a deeper scarlet), the new president had had more than enough. As he pulled himself up to his full stature (just over six feet), his measured words made his position quite clear: "Madam," he thundered during a meeting with members of the temperance lobby, "I may be the president of the United States, but what I do with my private life is my own damned business!"

A NEW YORKER, EH?

A longtime New Yorker, Arthur had a home on Lexington Avenue in Manhattan. As vice president, Arthur retreated to this home upon the attempt on President Garfield's life, and upon Garfield's death Arthur took the oath of office and became the twenty-first president of the United States. When Arthur was first nominated for vice president, there was unfounded speculation that he was born in Canada and therefore wasn't eligible for the position under the Constitution's natural-born-citizen clause. But he was, in fact, born in Vermont. In memory of this controversy, why not try a Canadian Manhattan?

Canadian Manhattan
3 oz. Canadian whisky
1 oz. sweet vermouth
1 cherry

Shake well with ice and strain into a cocktail glass. Garnish with cherry and serve.

Grant had left some outstanding vintages in the Executive Mansion cellar. Those exquisite bottles had, if anything, improved while slumbering through the Hayes administration. And President Arthur did not intend for them to remain corked and unloved forever.

THE JOCKEY CLUB MADEIRA

A frequenter of Delmonico's, Sam Ward (a.k.a. the "King of the Lobby") knew Arthur before he became president. As a successful lobbyist, Ward also knew how to entice politicians with luxurious gifts.

Apparently, one of the gifts he made to President Arthur included some bottles of old Madeira wine. These particular bottles were said to have been from South Carolina's Charleston Jockey Club. As the story goes, the Jockey Club had hundreds of bottles of aged, precious wine. But when General William Tecumseh Sherman approached the city in 1864 on his "March to the Sea," the aristocratic denizens of Charleston hid the best vintages. (Some supposedly were hidden in the basement of an insane asylum.) Decades later, much of the Jockey Club wine was sold off to cover debts. Sam Ward ended up with dozens of bottles. He saw fit to send some to Arthur as a gift, and, according to some accounts, these bottles of Madeira were stored in the Executive Mansion cellar, along with a note relating their storied history.

A CONTRARY VIEW

After he left the Executive Mansion in March 1885, Arthur returned to New York City with the intention of resuming his law career. But the onslaught of Bright's disease came on rapidly, and the former man-about-town spent the rest of his days cooped up in his Manhattan residence. The side effects of Bright's disease include lethargy and depression and a gradual wasting away of weight. Arthur's once large and robust frame was a memory during his final weeks of life, but by all accounts he faced his fate courageously.

In an interesting and contrary view, after Arthur's death in November 1886, Dr. George A. Peters (the former president's personal physician) felt compelled to state that Arthur's excesses with rich food and drink were exaggerated.

"The common impression that he was a high liver is a mistaken one," Peters told the *New York Times*. "He was never that in the sense in which it is applied to men who really live high." Of course, one's definition of "high living," especially in the Gilded Age, is relative.

LAST CALL ....

A friend of Arthur's once mentioned that a mutual acquaintance of theirs had been embarrassingly intoxicated. Rather than pry for details, Arthur emphatically stated: "No gentleman ever sees another gentleman drunk...."

BENJAMIN

HARRISON

★ 1889–1893 ★

"…A PLEASANT, CHEERFUL DINNER OF THE KIND
WHERE ONLY ENOUGH WINE IS TAKEN TO GIVE
VIVACITY TO THE MIND."

—Benjamin Harrison

A MODERATE TIPPLER

BENJAMIN HARRISON was the great-grandson of one of the signers of the Declaration of Independence and the grandson of "Old Tip," President William Henry Harrison. But he probably owed much more of his presidential success to the scheming of Pennsylvania politician Matthew Stanley Quay, who guided his campaign (and helped Harrison steal New York State) than to his distinguished historical pedigree.

In fact, Harrison bristled if people around him made too big a fuss about his famous ancestors; he wanted to be considered his own man, ascending to the Executive Mansion on his own merit—with a little assistance from God, perhaps.

Like many politicians of his era, emerging from the Civil War as an officer of high rank helped Harrison's credibility with voters in his home state of Indiana. The growing power of the temperance movement, however, was always a force (and potential source of votes) to be considered.

Therefore, like most savvy politicos of his era, Republican presidential candidate Harrison—en route to becoming the twenty-third president—did not go out of his way to showcase the moderate amounts of alcohol he consumed.

But considering that Harrison was both preceded and followed by known beer-lover Grover Cleveland, perhaps alcohol consumption was not such a detriment to political fortune as one might have imagined.

KING ALCOHOL VS.
THE TITANS OF TEMPERANCE

A decade before the Civil War, Harrison, a lawyer by trade, was already branching out into the political arena. He was once asked to share his views on temperance to a Hoosier crowd. The speaker before him apparently had already confessed that he had suffered the evils of drink before he saw the light. Fearing it might be a tough act to follow, Harrison more or less petitioned the crowd for a bit of understanding in advance because he was "inexperienced not only in making temperance speeches, but in drinking whiskey."

> ...for unlike the reformed drunkard who addressed you so powerfully, I can recount no life spent in the service of King Alcohol; nor can I speak of a home made desolate by its ravages.

All that said, Harrison (knowing his crowd) emphatically added that "drunken demagogues" should be ousted from legislative and judicial positions and their spots filled by "honest temperance men." Obviously he considered himself one of the latter. Harrison was not exactly a teetotaler, however.

WHISKEY WARRIORS

Harrison, a pious man, served as a general in the Civil War with the Seventieth Indiana Regiment and held prayer meetings at his tent. Harrison's letters from the field seem to hint that he drank a bit more than he might have as a civilian back home in Indiana, but those records also stress that his consumption was moderate. And they do not hide his disdain for his fellow officers (or even his superiors) who fell under the spell of Demon Alcohol.

When some of his fellow officers got their hands on some quality bourbon and knocked back a few measures, Harrison humorously penned to his wife Carrie: "Some of the officers got quite mellow and I laughed more than I did for a year before at the antics of some of them, particularly Col. Dustin."

But did the future president of the United States imbibe in a sip or two of the char-barreled nectar too? He allowed to his wife that he might have "touched it very lightly myself."

NO LOVE FOR HOOKERS

Harrison may have confessed to his own "light touch," but he was no fan of heavy-handed whiskey sluggers. When General Joseph "Fighting Joe" Hooker was appointed to a branch of the Union Army that included Harrison's Indiana unit, the future president was much chagrined. Writing to his wife in April 1864, Harrison feared that "whiskey....would be the ascendant now, if the stories about Hooker are well founded."

Some of those stories came from men very high up in President Lincoln's administration. As Secretary of the Navy Gideon Welles noted in his diary in 1863: "[Francis] Blair, who was present, said [Hooker] was too great a friend of John Barleycorn." And furthermore, Welles wrote:

> From what I have since heard, I fear [Hooker's] habits are not such to commend him, that at least he indulges in the free use of whiskey, gets excited, and is fond of play. This is the result of my inquiries....

Hooker's arrival also meant the reassignment of General Howard, a man who, like Harrison, was quite religious (and not a drinker). It was no wonder that Harrison viewed the switch as a lose-lose situation. To make matters worse, Hooker had a sidekick—General Ward—who also liked his liquor. Harrison refers to Ward in his writings as getting "beastly drunk" and also as a "lazy sot."

Like General George Washington, Harrison did not turn a blind eye when men below him mucked up the army's efficiency by lifting the whiskey jug. He once fired a regiment postmaster for chronic intoxication.

WHISKY FROM DEWAR'S

President Harrison was once the grateful recipient of a gift from industrial baron Andrew Carnegie. The gift from Scottish-born Carnegie was a cask of fine Scotch whisky from the John Dewar & Sons distillery. A Dewar's Fizz seems a fitting way to remember the days of the Harrison administration.

Dewar's Fizz
2 oz. Dewar's Scotch Whisky
1 tbsp. superfine sugar
1 oz. lemon juice
½ oz. lime juice
3 or 4 ice cubes
club soda

Combine all ingredients except the soda in a cocktail shaker and shake vigorously. Strain into a highball glass, fill with soda, and serve.

WHISKEY WARMTH

Nevertheless, Harrison knew that alcohol had both its charms and uses. Slogging through inclement weather on a march against the Confederates, Harrison was sympathetic to the plight of the rank-and-file soldier, as he mentioned to his wife:

> Some of the wagons did not get in until noon the next day and the rear guard was forced to stand all night in a swamp and without a fire to do any good. I went out four miles the next day and took a ration of whiskey to them.
>
> Last night when we and all our bed clothes were wet it turned cold and froze quite hard this morning. We got up stiff all over.

In contrast to the enlisted man's whiskey ration, Harrison—who enjoyed the occasional benefits of dining under more refined conditions—spoke to the attributes of moderation concerning "a pleasant, cheerful dinner of the kind where only enough wine is taken to give vivacity to the mind."

JOHN S. WISE WEIGHS IN

In his *Recollections of Thirteen Presidents*, John S. Wise had this take on Benjamin Harrison:

> He did indeed have two prominent traits of the Harrisons, for he was fond of shooting and a religious enthusiast.... He utterly lacked another family trait, for many of the Virginia branch have dearly loved whisky. My father, who knew them all and loved them, but had a way of saying what he pleased, generalized Harrison traits that he never knew a Harrison who was not a gentleman, but some were inclined to run to extremes—some in the love of God, and others in the love of whisky.

President Benjamin Harrison was quite "inclined" toward God (though he was not entirely unfamiliar with whiskey) and, in fact, gave the Lord great credit for his winning of the Executive Mansion. "Providence has given us the victory!" Harrison exclaimed to Republican chairman Senator Matthew Quay shortly after securing the 1888 election victory. In a cynical aside to a journalist, Quay blurted out: "Think of the man! He ought to know that Providence hadn't a damned thing to do with it...." Quay also said that Harrison would never know how many underlings had been "compelled to approach the gates of the penitentiary" in order to get him elected.

> ...[S]ome were inclined to run to extremes—some in the love of God, and others in the love of whisky.

CARNEGIE'S "CONGRESSIONAL" CARGO

Industrial magnate Andrew Carnegie loved to send casks of fine scotch whisky to people he deemed worthy. Mark Twain, for example, had long been a recipient of Carnegie's liquid kindness, once observing that it was "the smoothest whisky now on the planet."

As president of the United States, Harrison made the Carnegie gift list. Carnegie sent Harrison a keg of scotch from John Dewar & Sons, and (like Twain) the sender spoke most highly of its contents. The Scottish-born Carnegie must have also sent some sort of amusing message with the keg, because Harrison's thank-you note for the precious cargo mentioned: "It was very nice of you to think of me as to needing a 'brace' this winter in dealing with congress."

If Carnegie was pleased with sending the gift of Scottish spirits, and Harrison quite content to receive it, perhaps only Thomas R. Dewar (son of the distillery's deceased founder, John Dewar) outstripped them in his enthusiasm concerning the shipment.

"It was the very best kind of advertising I ever had and certainly the cheapest.... Inquiries and orders flowed to us from all parts of the States," said Dewar, once word spread concerning the delivery of whiskey to the Executive Mansion.

A few months after shipping Carnegie's keg, a traveling Dewar swung by the Executive Mansion, as he documented in his book *A Ramble Round the Globe*. Dewar did not get to meet President Harrison, but a tour guide showed him around:

> He was expatiating proudly on the fact that everything was American-made, when I mentioned that he must not forget that there is something from Scotland in the cellar. At first he looked hurt; but when I gave him my card, and he saw who I was, his countenance relaxed, and the meaning smile which beamed over it proved that he was as well aware as I of what had travelled from Perth to Washington, some months previously.

HARRISON'S ANCESTORS

Most presidential history buffs know that William Henry Harrison, Benjamin's grandfather, won the Executive Mansion on the infamous "Log Cabin and Hard Cider" campaign. But Benjamin Harrison—"Little Ben's" great-grandfather—most definitely fit John S. Wise's description of the family branch fond (in the extreme) of whiskey. The portly delegate from Virginia was one of the original signers of the Declaration of Independence, and was sometimes dubbed "The Falstaff of Congress."

LAST CALL

Special events at the Benjamin Harrison Presidential Home in Indianapolis have included a croquet tournament and a Civil War dinner—the latter accompanied by wine and a "guest" dressed up as General Benjamin Harrison. Confirmation is still pending on whether there might be a keg of Carnegie-sent scotch hidden somewhere on the site.

WILLIAM

McKINLEY

★ 1897–1901 ★

"WE CANNOT GAMBLE WITH ANYTHING
SO SACRED AS MONEY."

—William McKinley

ANOTHER CIVIL WAR— WET V. DRY

ONE CAN ARGUE that William McKinley lived through two Civil Wars: the bloody struggle between North and South and the emerging conflict between "wet" and "dry" factions that eventually led to the enactment of Prohibition.

Yet another president from Ohio, McKinley (the twenty-fifth president), knew that being a successful politician in the Midwest meant showing at least some deference to the temperance movement—if not actually completely embracing the teetotaler gospel.

McKinley himself was known to imbibe moderately, like most gentlemen of his day, enjoying a glass of wine with dinner and the occasional whiskey nightcap. Though he was unfortunately (and wrongly) mixed up with an unrelated boozer named John McKinley from the same regiment during the Civil War, future president William McKinley did in fact get a little tipsy at least once during his army days.

Despite, or because of, his own experiences in the Civil War, McKinley initially resisted the "war hawks" who were drumming up a reason to boot the Spanish out of Cuba. But he eventually gave way to pressure from the likes of Teddy Roosevelt (McKinley's second-term vice president) and Henry Cabot Lodge. The public's reaction to the sinking of the *Maine* in Havana Harbor provided the necessary tinder to touch off what some deemed "a splendid little war."

WHAT'S IN A NAME?

In one of his early elections, an 1876 contest for a U.S. congressional seat, McKinley had to fight off accusations that he had frequently been intoxicated during the Civil War. (McKinley rose to the officer ranks after he heroically risked his life at the Battle of Antietam, resupplying Union soldiers under intense fire at what is now known as the Burnside Bridge.) Two facts made McKinley's defense against these political snipes somewhat tricky. One, there had been another officer—a John McKinley (no relation to the future president, but also in the 23rd Ohio Regiment)—who did, in fact, get notoriously blasted. Soldiers fighting in the same theater of war might have easily associated the name McKinley with drinking binges.

> McKinley must have been the drunkest.

The second fact was a bit stickier. Though hardly a chronic boozer, William McKinley apparently had, on at least one occasion, drank to excess at a social reception hosted by General George Crook, in Cumberland, Maryland. The incident was recorded in a letter from Colonel James Comly to Colonel (and future president) Rutherford B. Hayes, who had been home on leave at the time. Comly wrote:

> ...a grand party. The belle of the evening was Chf.
> Quartermaster Farnsworth, who parts his hair in the
> middle. Gardner was the best dancer... and from
> what Kennedy tells me of the latter end of the thing,
> McKinley must have been the drunkest. I guess they
> had a little difficulty about it.

As for the *other* McKinley, Hayes wrote in his diary in 1862, lamenting that he had encouraged the sergeant to visit his homestead in Ohio while on leave:

> Heard from home. Sergeant [John] McKinley, with letter and watch—tight, drunk, the old heathen, and insisting on seeing the madame! I didn't dream of that. He must be a nuisance, a dangerous one too, when drunk. A neat, disciplined, well-drilled soldier under rule, but what a savage when in liquor! Must be careful whom I send home.

Given that description, it's no great surprise that Major William McKinley (despite whatever indiscretions he may have committed at Crook's ball) did not want to be mistaken for a chronic offender such as Sergeant McKinley. Hayes, the future president, had nothing but good to say about William McKinley, however, describing him in a letter home to his wife in December 1863 as "an exceedingly bright, intelligent, and gentlemanly young officer. He promises to be one of our best...."

MODERATE MCKINLEY

Although he was raised as a fairly strict Methodist, McKinley did have an occasional glass of wine with dinner and served wine to his guests at the Executive Mansion. He also often savored a glass of whiskey as a nightcap. But if McKinley had a true vice (if you can call it one), it was smoking cigars. He allegedly could smoke several dozen in one week and liked to enjoy them on a porch at the Executive Mansion, where he could not be readily observed.

McKinley obviously knew smoking was not the most healthful of habits. In fact, he did not like having his photograph taken while he had a cigar in hand or mouth, fearing that a president who smoked would set a bad example for the young men of America. He tried to be equally stealthy when it came to his moderate drinking habits.

MCKINLEY'S DELIGHT

McKinley—like most politicians of his day who weren't outright "dry" candidates—did his best to tap-dance around the alcohol issue. It must have been with mixed emotions, then, that—as the election of 1896 gathered steam—the Republican's most rabid supporters toasted him with concoctions dubbed "McKinley's Delight." The cocktail, supposedly created by a St. Louis barkeep during the 1896 GOP convention held there, is a basic Manhattan with a tweak or two. Sometime after the Spanish-American War, the drink's name morphed into "Remember the Maine." But regardless of its name, the recipe is something like this (below is a stronger, less sweet version):

McKinley's Delight/Remember the Maine
3 oz. rye whiskey (shoot for at least 100 proof)
1 oz. sweet vermouth
2 dashes of cherry brandy
1 dash absinthe

Shake it up, pour over ice. Serve in a double old fashioned glass.

CARNEGIE'S SECRET CARGO

As was his generous habit over several presidential administrations, industrial titan Andrew Carnegie relished supplying the Executive Mansion with a liquid gift—a barrel of scotch whisky, typically from the Dewar distillery in Scotland.

With "dry" sentiment in the country on the upsweep, most of the presidents who had terms that coincided with Carnegie's years tried to keep the steelmaker's generosity a secret, with varying success. At any rate, McKinley got his barrel of scotch from Carnegie, too, with instructions to pass it on to those who might appreciate it if the president did not want to keep it for his own consumption.

CARRIE "THE HATCHET" NATION VS. BREWERY BILL

Temperance advocate Carrie Nation—the volatile, hatchet-wielding nemesis of all things alcoholic—suspected that McKinley was a closet drinker and referred to him as "the brewer's president." Given McKinley's moderate habits, it seems a bit overstated, but Nation was not a matron given to compromise. She once destroyed a saloon painting depicting the Egyptian queen Cleopatra at the baths because she deemed it filth. She came back later and destroyed a good number of liquor bottles and was about to chop up the bar itself when local law enforcement intervened.

> He is a friend of the brewer and the drinking man.

Nation often toured the country and delivered her fiery spiel to what were typically receptive audiences. She happened to be speaking at Coney Island, New York, just days after McKinley's assassination in September 1901. While McKinley lingered near death, the hostile Nation dispensed not an ounce of sympathy concerning the president's grave condition. According to one news report, Nation bellowed: "Bill McKinley deserves to die. He is a friend of the brewer and the drinking man.... He deserves just what he got."

Hundreds in the crowd almost instantly booed and hissed at her, whereupon the reformer snarled back, referring to them as "hell hounds" and "snakes" and "sots." Nation's manager wisely hustled her off as some of the most hostile began to menacingly approach the speaker's stage. Soon after, the crowd broke out with three hearty cheers for McKinley.

LAST CALL ....

As a lawyer in Ohio, McKinley worked to stop the sale of liquor to students at Mount Union College. As president, McKinley once complained that he could not sip a glass of wine or touch a deck of cards without drawing fire in the press. After McKinley was shot by Czolgosz at the Pan American Exposition on September 6, 1901, whiskey and other stimulants were used in the president's treatment. A Kentucky distillery even sent bottles of their "best whiskey" to Buffalo—gratis—for McKinley's doctors to use in the unsuccessful effort. The twenty-fifth president lingered for a number of days before dying on September 14.

THEODORE

ROOSEVELT

★ 1901–1909 ★

"IT HAPPENS THAT I AM, AS REGARDS LIQUOR, AN
EXCEEDINGLY TEMPERATE MAN.... I NEVER TOUCH
WHISKY AT ALL AND I HAVE NEVER DRUNK A
HIGHBALL OR COCKTAIL IN MY LIFE. I DOUBT IF
I DRINK A DOZEN TEASPOONS OF BRANDY A YEAR."

—Theodore Roosevelt

THE RIGHT STUFF

TEDDY ROOSEVELT is often presented as a larger-than-life figure, with a dash of myth and majesty—and tongue-in-cheek braggadocio tossed in for good measure.

Roosevelt proponents, of course, can make a plausible case for their man being one of history's most noteworthy presidents, and a man who brought forth "the right stuff" long before he was in the White House. (The official "White House" name was established during TR's first year in office.)

He was the "Hero of San Juan Hill," leading his Rough Riders through the snap and buzz of projectiles; the man who challenged the corruption of New York, both city and state; the prolific author and winner of the Nobel Peace Prize; the man who finished a lengthy political speech while still bleeding from an assassin's bullet ("It takes more than a bullet to kill a Bull Moose!"); and the president who oversaw the building of the Panama Canal.

One might expect a man of Teddy Roosevelt's historical stature to have hoisted a few rounds in a gigantic silver goblet or something fittingly grandiose, but that's not how he rolled.

Drinking alcohol, it seems, was one of the few pursuits in which TR engaged on a rather modest scale. In fact, President Roosevelt was not only a moderate imbiber, but proud of it, too.

THE BRAWL-ROOM BLITZ

Adversaries—be they foreign powers or individuals attempting to intimidate him—underestimated Roosevelt at their own peril. Despite serious asthma issues that plagued him most of his life, TR robustly pursued physical activities, both indoor and out. One of his indoor specialties was boxing. The lessons learned in the gym apparently came in handy later in life.

In his autobiography, Roosevelt describes a confrontation with a drunken cowboy in a barroom on one of his many trips out West. His gun-wielding aggressor brazenly addressed TR as "four eyes" (a reference to his trademark spectacles) and insisted that Roosevelt would treat the locals to a round of drinks.

> Accordingly, in response to his reiterated command that I should set up the drinks, I said, "Well, if I've got to I've got to," and rose looking past him.
>
> As I rose, I struck quick and hard with my right just to one side of the point of his jaw, hitting with my left as I straightened out, and then again with my right. He fired the guns, but I do not know whether this was merely a convulsive action of his hands or whether he was trying to shoot at me. When he went down, he struck the corner of the bar with his head…and if he had moved I was about to drop on his ribs with my knees; but he was senseless.

There is a similar story of TR decking an antagonist—a rival Democratic politician named John Costello, who reportedly referred to Roosevelt as that "damned little dude"—in an Albany, New York, saloon. Roosevelt was a new representative in the New York State Assembly, but that did not prevent him from displaying his pugilistic skills when such obvious insults were hurled within earshot.

Curiously, Teddy does not mention this incident in his autobiography, but friends who witnessed it claimed that he ordered Costello to clean himself up—while lecturing him on how to behave when around gentlemen—and then insisted on buying the humiliated pol a peacemaking beer.

SELF-DESCRIBED ASS

If TR's offer to buy a round was a good gesture in the aftermath of the Albany affair, he was perhaps a bit overzealous when he wanted to buy a round—a rather big round, in fact—in San Antonio, Texas during training camp in 1898. The recipients of TR's generosity were the troopers of the First U.S. Volunteer Cavalry Regiment—the men who would become the much-storied Rough Riders of San Juan Hill fame during the Spanish-American War in Cuba.

In Roosevelt's defense, the weather in Texas in mid-May was already scorching and, therefore, quite capable of provoking a thirst which warm and fetid canteen water simply could not satisfy. After a mounted drill that they must have performed to TR's satisfaction, he sought to reward his men. Allowing them to dismount at the Riverside Fairgrounds, their leader festively announced that they could drink "all the beer they want, which I will pay for!"

This declaration obviously made Roosevelt quite popular with his Rough Riders. But his more experienced commander, Colonel Leonard Wood, knew the enthusiastic New Yorker might later regret this generosity. That evening Roosevelt was requested to appear before Wood, who sternly pointed out the potential pitfalls of rubbing shoulders with enlisted men, particularly when that fraternization was lubricated with alcohol. An embarrassed Teddy—in a rare moment of silence—snapped off a salute and then abruptly left headquarters. In a few minutes, however, he sheepishly returned before Wood and readily acknowledged his mistake: "Sir, I consider myself the damnedest ass within ten miles of this camp," declared the future president. "Good night, sir."

THE "BIG STICK" STRIKES IRON ORE

Although the young TR was not above buying drinks for others (except an intoxicated, pistol-toting cowboy), in his later years he

TR'S MINT JULEPS AND
THE TENNIS CABINET

Thanks to Archie Butt's keen observations, we have a good idea how Teddy Roosevelt had his courtside mint juleps prepared by White House steward Henry Pinckney. The president was "dee-light-ed" when they were served courtside to his guests—typically cabinet members or staffers who had been cajoled into playing tennis with him.

The main deviation from a southern-styled mint julep is that Teddy opted for rye whiskey instead of bourbon, and he added a splash of brandy. While no true Kentuckian would ever dream of using anything other than bourbon in this drink so tethered to Churchill Downs tradition, TR never had a problem with going his own way.

TR's Courtside Mint Juleps

10 to 12 fresh mint leaves "muddled" (until it resembles a paste) with a splash of water and a sugar cube
2 or 3 oz. rye whiskey
¼ oz. brandy
sprig or two of fresh mint as a garnish

First fill a collins glass with the muddled mint, then fill the glass generously with finely crushed ice. Top off with the rye whiskey, brandy, and mint garnish.

took great offense at the mere suggestion that he himself might be a hard drinker.

In 1913, an obscure newspaper in Michigan's Upper Peninsula—the Ishpeming *Iron Ore*—ran an editorial that outrageously claimed: "Roosevelt gets drunk, and that not infrequently, and all his intimates know it." Sick and tired of such attacks from small-minded, rumor-mongering "rags," Colonel Roosevelt (as the *New York Times* typically referred to him) launched a vigorous counterattack. The man who made the phrase "Speak softly and carry a big stick" famous also slammed George A. Newett, the editor of the paper, with a ten-thousand-dollar libel suit, with full intention of sending a message to other would-be character assassins. TR also traveled to Marquette County Courthouse in Michigan to testify at the trial in person.

Roosevelt's line of defense was not unlike the contents of a letter he once sent to William Hatfield Jr. when explaining his practice of controlled imbibing:

> It happens that I am, as regards liquor, an exceedingly temperate man. I drink about as much as Dr. Lyman Abbott—and I say this with his permission. I never touch whisky at all and I have never drunk a highball or cocktail in my life. I doubt if I drink a dozen teaspoons of brandy a year.

Dr. Abbott, a former pastor and theologian and one of TR's most trusted friends and allies, testified by letter that if Teddy drank too much of anything, that liquid might be milk. Other key witnesses (including some newspapermen who had covered Roosevelt during his political career) took the stand on TR's behalf—as did the former president himself. Teddy charmed the courtroom with his tales of adventure around the world, recounting the very occasional drinks he might have had.

After five days in court, Newett finally capitulated and admitted that he had been wrong to write an editorial claiming that Roosevelt was frequently drunk. TR did not offer to buy his foe a

HAT IN THE RING:
TR'S GRAND GARNISH

Upon his return from Africa in 1910, Roosevelt became increasingly disenchanted with President Taft, TR's former secretary of war. In fact, in February of 1912, Roosevelt announced he would run against Taft (and eventual Democratic winner Woodrow Wilson) thundering: "My hat is in the ring, the fight is on, and I am stripped to the buff!"

As if to honor the "hat in the ring" battle cry, a Chicago hotel/bar entrepreneur fashioned a drink in Teddy's honor. The drink ingredients in the "Teddy Hat" cocktail were nothing unusual:

Teddy Hat Cocktail:
1 oz. gin
½ oz. raspberry syrup
½ oz. dubonnet
several dashes orange bitters

Fill a bar glass with crushed ice. Add all ingredients. Shake vigorously and strain into a cocktail glass.

But it was the garnish that made this drink famous! As its name suggests, the lemon was cut into the shape of TR's famous Rough Rider hat and—with a bit of ceremony—tossed into the glass (i.e., the "hat in the ring").

conciliatory post-trial beer, but he did magnanimously drop his monetary damages down to the lowest allowable amount—a mere six cents. When reporters asked him what he might spend the six cents on, Roosevelt allegedly quipped that it was just enough for "a good paper." (The *Iron Ore* sold for half that price.)

THE MINT JULEP CAVEAT

Despite TR's sworn aversion to whiskey and claims that he never touched the stuff, there remains at least one contrary fact: he admitted a very occasional indulgence in mint juleps, made with fresh mint grown on the White House grounds. In the *Iron Ore* trial, the colonel allowed: "There was a fine bed of mint at the White House. I may have drunk a half dozen mint juleps in a year." Roosevelt's lawyer, the esteemed James H. Pound of Detroit, drew some hearty laughter from the packed courtroom when he asked TR: "Did you drink them all at once?"

Regardless of how many TR drank or when, the fact remains that a mint julep's primary fortification comes from whiskey—Kentucky bourbon, or whiskey not technically a bourbon. But TR's variation (mixed by White House steward Henry Pinckney) seems to have used several ounces of rye whiskey and a quarter ounce of brandy instead. So when the old Rough Rider said he "never" drank whiskey, a more accurate statement should have included "except when presented with fresh mint sprigs, a sugar cube, and finely crushed ice."

> Did you drink them all at once?

TENNIS AND POST-MATCH REFRESH-MINT

Had the *Iron Ore* editor's attorney had access to the letters of Colonel Archie Butt—Teddy Roosevelt's aide—he might have at least given the judge some pause. In various letters to his mother

A DRINK FIT FOR A ROUGH RIDER

Another cocktail in honor of TR had preceded the "Teddy Hat" in 1910 and was billed in the *Baltimore Sun* as "A New Roosevelt Cocktail." What the drink may have lacked in creative garnish, it more than made up for in alcoholic wallop (perhaps it should have been dubbed "The Big Stick Cocktail"), as its creator claimed it could motivate "a milksop" to "thrash a Rough Rider." The recipe looks like this:

New Roosevelt Cocktail
1 oz. San Juan Rum (dark)
½ oz. dry vermouth
½ oz. dry gin
a dash of absinthe
a dash of Kirschwasser

Pour ingredients into a shaker half-filled with ice. Shake well, stir into a cocktail glass, and serve.

and sister-in-law, Butt mentions that TR often liked to break out the mint juleps after a few sets of tennis—and he liked to play tennis, several days a week, rain or shine. As Butt noted (in a letter) after one particular match:

> It was a pleasant afternoon. He was in his best humour, and during the afternoon Longworth and his wife, Mr. Pinchot, the forester, and some others came in. The President had already ordered four mint juleps, but before they were served they had got up to eight. As each guest would arrive he would say to someone inside: "One more mint julep, please," and then laugh with glee. Finally, when they were served on the lawn by the side of the tennis court, he offered a toast to his new aide. "Wouldn't dear old Fairbanks [his VP, Charles W.] give a great deal to be able to sit down and enjoy one of these without fearing that a photograph fiend was hidden behind the bushes?" he said. "It is almost worth being called a drunkard by Wall Street to feel free to take a julep such as this without shocking the public."
>
> Just then Secretary Garfield [James R., son of the late president] said hurriedly: "Look out, here comes a sightseeing automobile by the White House."
>
> The President grabbed his glass, and with mock fear put it under the table.
>
> "That is the first evidence of fear I have ever seen in you, Mr. President," laughed the Secretary.
>
> "Not for my reputation, Garfield, but for you. After all Wall Street has said about me mine can't be injured, but you, my dear boy-faced Secretary, you may yet need the vote of the teetotaler."
>
> The juleps were certainly good, especially after the seven sets of tennis. The President and I finished ours first....

LAST CALL

TR aficionados who visit Washington and crave a drink might find Teddy & the Bully Bar near Dupont Circle just the place to go. There is plenty of TR-related art, as well as drinks dubbed "The Trust-Buster" and "The Rough Rider."

TAFT

★ 1909–1913 ★

"IT IS MY EXPERIENCE…THAT THE GOOD WOMEN OF
THE TEMPERANCE MOVEMENT ARE USUALLY TOTALLY
DEVOID OF HUMOR."

—William Howard Taft

A HEAVY HITTER

WILLIAM HOWARD TAFT loved being part of the judicial process, loved riding horses, really enjoyed playing golf (although he would have been no threat to make the PGA tour), and he absolutely loved eating. (At just under six feet tall, Taft's weight peaked at 340 pounds.)

But it would be a stretch to say he liked being president very much. When his bid to return to the White House failed in 1912, it cleared the way for Taft to get a position he truly relished: chief justice of the United States Supreme Court. Presidential trivia buffs might note that Taft is the only man to serve both as president (the nation's twenty-seventh) and chief justice (the tenth).

In the months after leaving the White House, Taft was able to bring his weight down to a self-reported 270; not a bad effort, but one that he said required abstention from all alcohol, potatoes, and fatty meats, such as pork. No doubt removing the stress of being president helped, too.

Theodore Roosevelt more or less groomed Taft—his secretary of war and fellow Republican—to be his presidential successor in the election of 1908. TR advised Taft on how to deal with the growing power of the temperance movement. TR's strategy was essentially to avoid all contact with the teetotalers, if possible—the message, seemingly, was that there would be political points to be lost, and few to be gained, by any messy confrontations.

BIG BOOZER...OR BIG SNOOZER?

William Howard Taft looks like a guy with whom one would like to hoist a few. His walrus-like appearance, considerable girth, and natural affability all seem to suggest that he would be quite at home grasping a sweating glass with a large paw. Can you picture Taft wearing an extra-extra-large T-shirt advertising some surf shop, bellying up at a thatched-roof beach bar for some magically mixed, rum-laced cocktail in a glass made to look like a coconut?

Absolutely! But it would not be true. William Howard Taft—despite his considerable bulk (requiring a specially sized bathtub to accommodate him in the White House)—must, when it comes to alcohol consumption, be considered a mere lightweight.

While all the evidence shows that Taft was not a big boozer, he was (apparently without the help of alcohol) a big snoozer. Much to the embarrassment of his staff, Taft would sometimes fall asleep at inopportune moments—such as funerals or public performances, or even while sitting in a chair waiting for an appointment.

ARCHIE BUTT WEIGHS IN

The presidential aide Archibald Butt summed up Taft's attitude toward alcohol in a letter to his sister-in-law, Clara. Butt could not fathom that the boredom of political life could be endured without at least *some* alcohol, noting:

> The President never takes anything to drink at all, but is most profligate in making others imbibe. I do not see how he sits through these long dinners and banquets without taking enough to merely exhilarate him, but he takes no alcoholic liquors of any kind and seems to be the better for it.

Along the lines of "making others imbibe," Butt mentioned that one of the less pleasant aspects of working for Taft was that the president would occasionally trap him to share in some boring political meeting—using scotch (which Taft knew Butt loved) as bait. As he lamented to Clara of a 1910 incident:

> Saturday night [in Albany] when he and Governor Hughes sat down in the library after coming in from a late banquet, I tried to slip upstairs and get to bed, for I was worn out; but he saw my maneuver, I think, for he said: "Governor, I am sure Captain Butt would like a Scotch and soda with you," and he made a motion for me to remain, so down I sat and never got up again for two hours and did not get to bed until after half-past two.

THE GREAT CHAMPAGNE SWITCH

President Taft instructed Colonel Butt to buy some of the best French champagne for guests at a dinner celebrating the passing of the controversial Payne-Aldrich Tariff Act. Butt, however—concluding that many attendees might not fully appreciate the good stuff—served run-of-the-mill bubbly to most of the guests. A chosen few were to be served the superior wine. (Note: this was decades before the term "Pulling a Nixon" came into the vocabulary of presidential history buffs.)

But a problem arose when Congressman Nicholas Longworth (who was married to TR's eccentric daughter, Alice) deduced this slight-of-hand. As Archie related to his sister-in-law in a letter:

> I was sitting next to Nick Longworth, and to my horror I noticed that the waiter, in serving the wine, passed me by and filled up Longworth's glass and later came back to serve me from the vintage wine, which I had not told him to do. I was drinking Scotch and soda. I loathe the taste of champagne. Nick promptly fired an arrow into the sky in the shape of a remark that I was serving two kinds of wine and possibly palmed off inferior brands on the unsuspecting.

Butt recovered enough to laugh off the accusation and ordered the waiter to keep Longworth's glass brimming with the good stuff. This seemed to satisfy the suspicious politician, much to Archie's relief, as he declared: "I never would have heard the last of it."

NO-BRAWL BILL

Residing in Cincinnati (one of the country's famous beer-brewing cities, along with Milwaukee and St. Louis), young Bill Taft appears to have visited the "Over-the-Rhine" section of the Queen City. This German section of Cincinnati was, of course, brimming with breweries and beer gardens. But according to one of Taft's earliest and most prolific biographers, Henry F. Pringle, the future president was quite moderate when it came to alcohol—even after he graduated from Yale and attended the University of Cincinnati College of Law.

> Taft... suggested to his companions that they leave before beer bottles started to fly.

> [Taft and his friends] went to the beer gardens, which abounded in the section called "Over the Rhine," across the canal. They would have dinner with beer or wine and enjoy the music. One night, during the 1880 campaign, some politicians began to argue vociferously...Taft reached for the check and suggested to his companions that they leave before beer bottles started to fly.

Similarly, Taft—again according to Pringle—seems to have been low-key at Yale, despite the fact that he was a member of the Skull and Bones fraternity. He is described as "a model young man" who did not smoke and drank "only an occasional glass of beer." And furthermore, he declined to tag along with "rowdy youths who broke loose, from time-to-time, and cavorted through the streets of New Haven."

BRONX COCKTAILS IN ST. LOUIS

A brief campaign shake-up emerged during a 1911 road trip to the western states. In St. Louis, the Taft contingent was treated to a breakfast that included something called "Bronx cocktails"—a brunch with an alcoholic punch, if you will. Though it is doubtful that Taft indulged, teetotaler forces in Missouri labeled the gathering as something of an outrage. Among other things, they surmised that there must have been whiskey in those Bronx cocktails.

The *New York Times* rose to the occasion to the defense of President Taft in an article on September 24, 1911, launching a counterattack against the Missouri ministers and their anti-alcohol crusaders. Put forth the *Times*:

> An annoying feature of President Taft's journey through the West has been the controversy caused by the presence of Bronx cocktails at a breakfast party he attended. One does not have to be a clergyman or a total abstainer to reprehend the practice of drinking cocktails before breakfast. The Taft breakfast, however, was in St. Louis and was really dejeuner, but that word is not tolerated in Missouri. It is not the time of day that seems so objectionable, but the mere fact of the controversy. When this Republic grows older, and mellows a little, such controversies will not be conducted in public....
>
> One preacher, for example, declared that a Bronx cocktail contains whisky.... So for a large part of Missouri from this time forward, the Bronx cocktail will contain whisky.
>
> So far as that particular cocktail is concerned, or, indeed, any other concoction of that type, we do not

CUBAN REFRESHMENT

Taft held many lofty positions in the U.S. in addition to the presidency. He was the chief justice of the Supreme Court, secretary of war, a circuit court judge, and solicitor general of the United States. Also, he was the first provisional governor of Cuba, during the second American occupation of the island nation. While he only held the position for two weeks, hopefully he was able to partake of the refreshing beverage named for the battle cry during Cuba's battle for independence in 1898—eight years prior to Taft's governorship.

Cuba Libre

2½ oz. light rum
6 oz. cola
juice of one half lime
1 lime wedge for garnish

Pour the rum and lime juice into a cocktail shaker half full of ice. Shake well and strain into a tall, ice-filled glass. Add the cola, stir, add the lime wedge, and serve.

care; it is the deplorably deficient culture of our country that depresses us....

Can it be that these Missouri clergymen are not college men? Anyhow, there is no whisky in a Bronx cocktail.

Although the Bronx cocktail seems rarely to get a mention these days, it is worth noting that it was typically composed of gin, with perhaps a little bit of vermouth and orange juice worked into the formula. And, unlike the fire and brimstone dispensed by the Missouri clergymen, the Bronx cocktail should be served up icy cold.

INTOXICATING TROUT

Before a political rift in 1912 pushed them apart, Taft and Teddy Roosevelt were good friends and political comrades-in-arms. TR, in fact, put all his might behind Taft's election (the big fellow was something of a reluctant draftee) in 1909. One of TR's strategies that Taft often employed was to avoid, whenever possible, any meeting with radical factions of the women's temperance movement, such as the hatchet-wielding Carrie Nation.

But once when Taft was on a swing through Colorado, he was ambushed—somewhat sweetly—by a contingent of Women's Christian Temperance Union (WCTU) sister-soldiers when he stepped off a train in Glenwood Springs. They were waiting for the hulking president with, of all things, a platter of trout that they wished to present to him. Seeing no chance to follow the strategy of the Hero of San Juan Hill (i.e. run away!), Taft could not resist "tweaking" the WCTU ladies. Were the women absolutely sure these trout were completely free of all intoxicants?

The stern-faced women assured the president that the trout were sans intoxicants—after all, they were total abstainers! When Taft had safely returned to the train, he turned to a traveling companion (a Bishop Brewster, no less) and stated, with a tight-but-knowing smile: "It is my experience... that the good women of the temperance movement are usually totally devoid of humor."

> William Howard Taft is the father
>
> of modern Bourbon Whiskey.

WHOA, NELLIE!

If Taft was restrained when it came to alcohol, his wife Helen "Nellie" Taft more than made up for it. Her diaries and letters even from her teen years are laced with references to her drinking, with beer (acquired in the beer gardens of Cincinnati's German "Over-the-Rhine" section), cocktails, and champagne leading the list.

On her 1888 honeymoon to Europe, for example, Nellie declared: "It seems impossible to go through Germany without drinking beer... I am very fond of it. What they call Pilsner is delicious." Once in the White House, Nellie drew some flak from the WCTU by serving champagne punch to the diplomatic corps. But she had no intention of letting them ruin her fun. She also played cards in the White House, sometimes even on a Sunday.

A stroke in 1909 temporarily slowed down the first lady. But if there was a health risk that made Nellie susceptible to stroke, the culprit was arguably her other vice—smoking cigarettes. She managed to rebound to a great degree and lived until 1943.

THE BOURBON HALL OF FAME

On December 17, 2009, some of the leaders of the art of making Kentucky bourbon flocked to the Old Governor's Mansion in Frankfort to honor—and toast—William Howard Taft. Since we know that Taft was not a whiskey drinker, one might find Big Bill a curious choice for the Kentucky Bourbon Hall of Fame. But, according to bourbon whiskey expert/historian Michael Veach, Taft deserved the honor because of the "Taft Decision" on whiskey that the president offered on December 27, 1909. Taft's legislation essentially answered the serious question of "What is Whiskey?"

The Taft Decision defined the various whiskey categories—"Straight," "Blended," and "Imitation"—that the distilling industry still utilizes. As Veach noted in his Filson Historical Society blog:

> Kentucky is the state that made the decision necessary because before this decision people would move to Kentucky and rectify a product and call it "Kentucky Bourbon" because they made it in Kentucky even if it had no aged whiskey in it at all. Because of this decision, William Howard Taft is the father of modern Bourbon Whiskey.

LAST CALL

Taft was in Montreal in 1921 when he got the word of his appointment to chief justice—a position he had always longed for—and, in a rare fit of jubilation, toasted his accomplishment with a glass of champagne.

The steel-mill tycoon Andrew Carnegie once sent Taft a case of scotch whisky, thinking that he might need a restorative swig during the 1912 election.

Nellie Taft recovered from her stroke and, in her golden years, traveled to Mexico, where, armed with the word "cerveza" (beer), she reportedly had a fine time.

WARREN G.

HARDING

★ 1921–1923 ★

"I HAVE NO TROUBLE WITH MY ENEMIES. I CAN
TAKE CARE OF MY ENEMIES ALL RIGHT. BUT MY DAMN
FRIENDS...THEY'RE THE ONES WHO KEEP ME WALKING
THE FLOOR NIGHTS!"

—Warren G. Harding

A "DRY" POL WHO
LOVED TO DRINK

A BAN ON the "transportation of intoxicating liquors" was one of several restrictions outlined in Prohibition. But not everyone followed the letter of that law. One of the flagrant flouters of the law was the twenty-ninth president, Warren Harding, who had no reservations about transporting a bottle of whiskey in his golf bag around the links at Chevy Chase and pausing to enjoy an occasional pop.

Harding is often listed as one of the worst presidents, mostly because of the Teapot Dome scandal, which involved blackmail, bribery, perjury, suicide, whispers of murder, and prison terms. But by the time it happened, Harding had already died (at the Palace Hotel in San Francisco on August 2, 1923, probably of heart failure).

Harding gave the appearance of being a "dry" politician, and Prohibition was solidly in place when he moved into the White House in 1920. But as socialite Evalyn McLean noted: "I knew that Warren Harding was counted as a dry senator, but that in moments of relaxation he was ready to drink.... Indeed I often heard him boast that he could make a champagne cocktail just like the Waldorf bartender." Perhaps a first-rate bartender, Harding was quite over his head in the White House, as he himself admitted. Colonel Edmund Starling, head of the Secret Service detail, remarked: "He was ruined by his friends, just as Wilson was ruined by his enemies. But the main point is, he should never have been President of the United States."

THE BIG FOUR

Warren G. Harding loved golfing, gambling (particularly poker), chasing women (other than his wife, Florence "The Duchess" Kling Harding), and drinking. Harding used alcohol to enhance the other three activities, though his friends maintained that he rarely consumed liquor to excess.

In fact, it seems that Harding may have enjoyed incredible tolerance. Harry Daugherty, Harding's savvy campaign manager, once brought the 1920 presidential long shot to *New York Times* reporter Arthur Krock's room at Washington's Willard Hotel for a drink prior to the Gridiron Club dinner. As Krock noted in his memoirs:

> I had imported a couple of bottles of rare prewar
> bourbon from Kentucky and, as I recall, the Senator
> from Ohio drank almost a pint by himself. Hang-
> over, he showed it not at all. He held his liquor well.

Warren Harding had no qualms about drinking in the White House (especially if cards were flicking around the poker table), but he also found the golf course a convenient place to imbibe. Early in his term, President Harding liked to take a pop in between holes from a bottle stashed in his golf bag. But at some point (perhaps on the advice of his aides) he decided a little discretion was in order; the president would wait until the rounds were over, then have a whiskey with his cronies in the confines of the clubhouse.

As Colonel Starling remarked:

> He played most often at the Chevy Chase Club, and
> used the house set aside for the President. I kept the
> key to the desk drawer where three or four bottles of
> Scotch and Bourbon were stored. When we returned
> to the house the colored man in attendance, Taylor,
> brought set-ups, and while the players drank high-
> balls I calculated the results of the bets and
> announced the winners. The President took a single

drink, and when this was finished and the bets were
settled he would say to me, "Telephone the Duchess
and say I am on my way home."

If his golf scores were any indication, Harding had reason to
drink. He often played twice a week, but even breaking one hundred sometimes proved a challenge for him. But nobody could
doubt his love of the game—he would play even on rainy days.

While Harding enjoyed playing at Chevy Chase, he was under
even less scrutiny when he golfed on the links that adjoined
"Friendship"—the estate of William "Ned" McLean and his
eccentric wife, Evalyn. McLean was a hard-drinking tycoon who
owned the *Washington Post* and eventually became ensnared in the
Teapot Dome fiasco.

In the wonderfully engaging book *First off the Tee: Presidential Hack-
ers, Duffers, and Cheaters from Taft to Bush*, Don Van Natta Jr. relates a
story from Shirley Povich, who caddied for Harding when Povich
was just seventeen. Three-quarters of a century after the fact,
Povich (who later became a renowned sports writer and editor at
the *Post*) recounted:

> "I showed up at the first tea and McLean was glad to
> see me.... He turned to the man standing with him
> and said 'Mr. President, this is Shirley Povich, the
> best caddy in America,' which was untrue. 'He's going
> to caddie for you today'." Shortly after the introduc-
> tions were made, Povich recalled that he was sur-
> prised to see butlers arrive with the afternoon's first
> round of drinks. And—to hell with Prohibition!—
> President Harding took a glass and a gulp. Imagine
> that.

Imagine that, indeed. Harding's love of golf also provided him
an excuse to avoid the Duchess and indulge in drinking and
gambling.

THE WHITE HOUSE SPEAKEASY

The Harding White House was relatively careful about alcohol in the downstairs floors. But it was another matter upstairs, where, if invited, one could count on a cocktail, a card game, or lots of both. Alice Roosevelt Longworth—Teddy Roosevelt's eccentric daughter renowned for unleashing her barbed witticisms against those around her, friend or foe—gave one of the most widely circulated accounts of what the White House social life was really like during Harding's term. In her memoir *Crowded Hours*, so-called "Princess Alice" wrote with thinly veiled disdain:

> No rumor could have exceeded the reality; the study was filled with cronies, [U.S. Attorney General Harry] Daugherty, Jess Smith, Alex Moore, and others, the air heavy with tobacco smoke, trays with bottles containing every imaginable brand of whisky stood about, cards and poker chips at hand—a general atmosphere of waistcoat unbuttoned, feet on the desk, and spittoons along side.

White House staffer Elizabeth Jaffray observed similar behaviors during the Harding years, stating:

> President Harding was the only man during the four administrations that I lived at the White House who drank enough to speak of. It was also [his] habit when he entertained me.... to retire after dinner to the library or study to play cards and have Scotch and soda served.

Colonel Starling claimed that Harding drank only moderately when playing. "At card games he drank one highball, then switched to ale," he said. But Starling stops short of saying how many ales Harding might have downed.

THE FIRST LADY AS BARMAID

First Lady Florence Harding did not appreciate a lot of her husband's habits—not only Warren's pursuit of other women but also his golfing and horseback riding, both of which he sometimes used as an excuse to skip church. However, the president often let her attend some of his poker games. But the Duchess was not there solely to kibitz; she had actual duties—such as serving drinks to Harding and his Ohio Gang cohorts.

One might find it difficult to imagine other first ladies (Jacqueline Kennedy? Rosalynn Carter? Pat Nixon? Hillary Clinton? Michelle Obama?) scurrying about to fetch alcohol for their husband's cronies—hunched over a poker table, wafts of cigar smoke curling around them. But the Duchess performed this task diligently and proficiently, even absorbing some good-natured abuse in the bargain.

As Alice Roosevelt Longworth commented:

> Harding and Nick [Senator Longworth, Alice's big-boozing husband] and the others would say when they wanted another drink, "Duchess, you are lying down on your job." And Mrs. Harding, who was watching the play of hands, would obediently get up and mix a whisky and soda for them.

THE CHINA SYNDROME

Lowlights in the Harding administration spring up like so many weeds on the White House lawn. That Harding once lost a set of White House china in a "cold hand" of poker is not the worst of it, but it does underscore how presidential dignity was relegated to the back seat during his Roaring Twenties term.

Whether Warren G. was slightly intoxicated on a highball and ale chasers, somewhat smitten with his female adversary, or both, is difficult to ascertain. But as the story goes, Harding impulsively bet attractive socialite Mrs. Louise Cromwell Brooks that he could deal a better "cold" hand than she—and offered up some fine china as his stake. Harding lost. The next day, boxes of

A DRINK ON THE LINKS

President Harding loved to play golf—and to sneak a few sips at the same time, despite Prohibition. He was known to throw back a few with the boys at the tony Chevy Chase Club in suburban Maryland, and doubtless would have appreciated a drink by the same name.

Chevy Chase
1½ oz. gin
1½ oz. dry vermouth
1½ oz. sweet vermouth
1 dash orange juice
1 dash orange bitters
¼ tsp. brandy

Combine all the ingredients in a cocktail shaker filled with ice and then stir well. Strain into a chilled cocktail glass and serve.

china—stamped with an imprint from President Benjamin Harrison's term—arrived at Mrs. Brooks's Massachusetts Avenue townhouse.

TRADING SHOTS WITH THE UNIONS

When the railroad unions went on a national strike in 1922, Harding played hardball with them in a meeting at the White House. This was not Harding's preferred style—he typically attempted to be friends with everybody and not rock the political canoe.

> ....Harding may have been intoxicated during the confrontation...

But knowing that the clash with union leaders was likely to be "no holds barred," Harding might have first resorted to some liquid courage. Union representatives later claimed that Harding was drinking shots of whiskey straight from the bottle (though, in all fairness, this does not sound like Harding's suave style) and slurring his words. Rabblerousing union speakers repeated the charges at a rally in Buffalo, New York, in the days following the White House meeting.

According to a 1998 *Washington Post* article, FBI records released in the 1990s also reported that a fired-up Harding may have been intoxicated during the confrontation with union officials. Regardless, the result was that the unions eventually caved, and the railroads were soon running again.

BABES AND BOOZE

The Harding legacy started to go to pieces just a few years after he died, when one of his former mistresses—Nan Britton—published a scandalous memoir about how the twenty-ninth president fathered a daughter out of wedlock with her. Titled *The President's Daughter*, it was considered dynamite in its day, and there were attempts to suppress it. Those attempts failed, however, and it eventually sold ninety thousand copies.

His alleged mistress recounted how she once sent him out from a hotel room in search of a bottle of champagne ("I guess I was a bit shy with him, and a glass of champagne made me a bit more talkative and revealing...."):

> Of course, Prohibition had already gone into effect, but I was told it was possible still to obtain liquor or wines if one knew how to do so and evidently Mr. Harding thought he did.... But when Harding returned, he sheepishly admitted: "No, dearie, I couldn't get it."

LAST CALL

Evalyn McLean owned a pet monkey that once snatched a bottle of lemonade at a party, scurried up ivy vines and trellises to a lofty perch on the side of the grand mansion, and then—from a great height—splashed most of its contents down on Warren G. Harding's fine-tailored suit. Perhaps it is a fitting metaphor for Harding's presidency, but one somehow wishes the mischievous monkey had been sufficiently armed with a full bottle of whiskey.

CALVIN

COOLIDGE

★ 1923–1929 ★

"To live under the American Constitution is the greatest political privilege that was ever accorded to the human race."

—Calvin Coolidge

SOBER
SILENT CAL

CALVIN "SILENT CAL" COOLIDGE rose to the presidency when Warren Harding met his untimely demise in 1923. When the news of Harding's death reached the powerful senator Henry Cabot Lodge, he was said to have blurted out: "Good God! Coolidge is president!"

Coolidge's term was largely uneventful, though he gets high marks today from those who champion fiscal discipline and less government. There were no wars to fight (other than the unpopular and clumsy one against bootleggers that the government was losing) and the Great Depression was yet to come.

When it came time to commit to a second term, Coolidge said: "I choose not to run...." But there are some historians who believe Cal was simply being coy—that he really wanted the Republican Party to plead for him to run. They did not. Instead, they hitched up Herbert Hoover—whom Coolidge sometimes facetiously referred to as "The Wonder Boy" or "The Great Engineer"—to the GOP wagon.

If Coolidge drank in the White House, he did so rarely. Calvin was a flyweight when it came to drinking alcohol. But when the great Wall Street Crash came in 1929, perhaps even "Cool Cal" contemplated a shot and a beer chaser—if for no other reason than to thank Fate that he was retired in New England and Hoover was the one who would be taking the heat.

JUST AN UNEXCITABLE BOY

Coolidge was, to put it mildly, not an electrifying personality. When he died, writer Dorothy Parker—supreme wielder of rapier witticisms—allegedly deadpanned: "How could they tell?" Alice Roosevelt Longworth dismissively remarked that Coolidge looked like someone "sucking on a pickle." Baltimore writer H. L. Mencken harvested great hay during the Harding-Coolidge-Hoover era; he could not take cynical aim at the targets fast enough. Mencken described Coolidge as "a stubborn little fellow with a tight, unimaginative mind"—and that was one of his less-malicious lines.

> Once every blue moon he... took a single, solemn glass of beer....

Of course Dorothy Parker, "Princess Alice," and H. L. Mencken all liked to drink. Coolidge, apparently, could take it or leave it—leaning most decidedly toward the latter. But did he ever? The best answer might be: very occasionally and with minimal consumption. William Allen White, one of Coolidge's earliest biographers, wrote in 1925:

> Once every blue moon he sat down in one of the gardens of Northampton [Massachusetts, where Coolidge once served briefly as mayor], took a single, solemn glass of beer—this was, of course, before the great Volstead drought—cracked a single, solemn joke, drier than the pretzel that he munched, and felt that he had for that day and season done his full social duty to God and man.

Suffice it to say, Coolidge was not a man destined to put a dent in the nation's grain production.

THE BARRISTER OF BREW

There was, however, a time in Coolidge's career when he championed those who did use up a lot of grain: the Springfield Brewery. This was early in Coolidge's lawyering career (1909 or so), but as biographer White suggested, it most likely helped him win the mayor's race in Northampton.

Among Coolidge's clients was the Springfield Brewery, and it was his business to look after its barkeeps in the courts. Sometimes he appeared for its drunks in the police court. Coolidge locked up the "wet" vote in Northampton, but he did his best not to antagonize the block of "dry" voters. And so he won the mayor's race. Not long after, he became the lieutenant governor and then governor of Massachusetts—and a tough-acting one who broke the Boston Police Strike. Then, despite it being such an obvious mismatch of personalities, Coolidge latched on as VP on the long shot (but ultimately winning) Harding ticket in 1920.

PECKING ORDER

Nothing lasts forever, and neither, apparently, did Teddy Roosevelt's precious bed of White House mint. In his book *42 Years in the White House*, Irwin "Ike" Hoover, the long-serving White House usher, wrote that President Coolidge once received a gift of two dozen chickens. Coolidge turned the birds loose in TR's mint bed—the very same bed that Colonel Roosevelt once plucked to make his special mint juleps after a few hotly contested sets of tennis. The chickens pecked away, and, when they were later consumed, Ike Hoover claimed the meat had a definite hint of mint to it. "We never knew whether [Coolidge] selected the mint bed on purpose or not," mused Hoover. "If he did, it was in keeping with many other odd things the President was up to."

REASONABLE DOUBT?

Arguably one of the most bizarre stories about Coolidge involves not chickens, but whiskey. The accomplished and prodigious presidential historian Richard Norton Smith unveiled this little

THE COOLIDGE COOLER

Just a few years ago, an American maker of vodka—Vermont Spirits—suggested that imbibers could use their product to make something called a "Coolidge Cooler"—preferably to be concocted on July 4, Silent Cal's birthday. The suggested recipe (with whiskey optional) is this:

Coolidge Cooler
1 ½ oz. Vermont White vodka
½ oz. American whiskey
2 oz. orange juice
club soda

Mix vodka, whiskey, and orange juice over ice. Top with club soda and serve.

> Ex-presidents have nothing left to do but get drunk.

gem in his 1990 book *An Uncommon Man: The Triumph of Herbert Hoover*. Smith writes that, according to some White House staffers, Coolidge, stung by the Republican Party's embrace of Hoover, trudged off to his room on the day of that announcement with a bottle of Green River whiskey clutched in his hand.

While whiskey drinking seems wildly out of character for Coolidge, the fit of pouting and pique does not. And perhaps Franklin Pierce's alleged adage—that ex-presidents have nothing left to do but get drunk—resonated with a brooding and possibly depressed Coolidge.

THE TOKAY RUSE

After Coolidge left the White House and Hoover (Herbert, not Ike!) took over, Cal and Mrs. Coolidge traveled across the country. One special stop was the sweeping Hearst Castle in San Simeon, California. At the majestic estates, publishing magnate William Randolph Hearst felt he should offer the ex-president a cocktail. Coolidge promptly reminded Hearst that he did not drink. As related in McCoy's *Calvin Coolidge: The Quiet President*, Hearst slyly attempted the host's equivalent of the quarterback sneak.

> "Neither do I," the publisher replied. "But I find that a sip of wine is an excellent appetizer."
>
> The former president asked: "Is it alcoholic?"
>
> "Not perceptibly," Hearst said. "The alcohol content is slight."

Hearst finally talked Cool Cal into a small glass of Tokay wine. Coolidge drank it. Then he accepted a second glass (virtually binge-drinking for Coolidge!) and remarked that he must remember what he drank for future reference.

LAST CALL

While it seems doubtful that Coolidge would have indulged in the "Coolidge Cooler," if the Green River whiskey story is true, then anything is possible.

HERBERT

HOOVER

★ 1929–1933 ★

"KEEP A BOTTLE OF WHISKEY IN YOUR BOTTOM
DRAWER AND AFTER THE DAY IS OVER, WHEN YOU'RE
TIRED AND BEFORE YOU START HOME, TAKE A
SWIG... AND IT WILL PEP YOU UP."

—Herbert Hoover

THE WONDER BOY

IF TIMING IS EVERYTHING, then Herbert Hoover looked totally out of sync by the end of his one disastrous term in the presidential office. The Republicans had won handily in 1928, promising "a chicken in every pot and a car in every garage" and predicting that poverty was on the brink of banishment in America. But when the stock market crashed and the Great Depression struck in 1929, the euphoria evaporated rapidly. Banks folded, bread lines and "Hoovervilles" formed, and the populace could not (at least not legally) even console itself with a shot or a beer, since Prohibition was still the law of the land.

As the thirty-first U.S. president limped toward the finish line at the end of his term, it seemed unlikely that he could beat the Democratic nominee, Franklin Delano Roosevelt. And, of course, he did not.

With just a few days left in Hoover's term, journalist Agnes Meyer wrote (on February 25, 1933) in her diary: "Hard on H. to go out of office to the sound of crashing banks. Like the tragic end of a tragic story.... The history of H's administration is Greek in its fatality."

Once billed as "The Wonder Boy," Hoover had now become associated with another word that rhymed with "wonder." As Meyer admitted: "God knows I wished him well. Looking back it seems like nothing but blunder after blunder...."

GONE, BABY, GONE

A graduate of Stanford, Hoover (prior to his political career) made good money as a mining engineer in Australia and China. His successes allowed him to enjoy some of the luxuries of life. For example, when Hoover resided in California, he possessed a quality wine cellar, including some well-aged port.

But when Prohibition came into effect, his wife, Lou Henry Hoover (a non-drinker) got rid of it all—apparently without even consulting Herbert. The rules of Prohibition would have allowed Hoover to keep his liquid stash, though transporting it somewhere else was technically against the law.

But that was a moot point once Lou dumped it all. Probably less than thrilled about this radical move, Hoover nevertheless managed to mutter something like: "I don't have to live with the American people, but I do have to live with Lou."

GOING THROUGH THE MOTIONS

Unlike the Warren G. Harding era, there was no cheating in the Hoover White House when it came to Prohibition. Dinner guests might have had experienced a jolt of hope when they saw dinner staff circling the table with bottles wrapped in towels, but it was not to be. The towels did not conceal a fabulous bottle of French champagne or a California red. While the ceremonial flourish suggested something stronger, surely the majority of guests were dismayed to find White Rock mineral water gurgling into their glasses.

A BRONX CHEER IN PHILLY

Hoover had once referred to Prohibition as "a noble experiment," but the president did not have to do anything more than venture out among the working class (many of them unemployed) to get the hint that the "experiment" was failing miserably.

When Hoover attended a World Series game between the St. Louis Cardinals and the hosting Philadelphia Athletics at Shibe Park in October 1931, a vocal section of the crowd—aware of the president's presence—began to jeer: "We want beer! We want beer!"

To make matters worse, Hoover received bad news during the game. He and the first lady got up to leave in the eighth inning, but—as he later recorded somberly in his memoirs—the crowd once again proved rudely hostile:

> I was not able to work up much enthusiasm over the ball game and in the midst of it I was handed a note informing me of the sudden death of [New Jersey] Senator Dwight Morrow. He had proven a great pillar of strength in the Senate and his death was a great loss to the country and to me. I left the ballpark with the chant of the crowd ringing in my ears: "We want beer!"

H. L. MENCKEN'S BARBED-WIRE WORDS

If Hoover was unable to dodge the frustrated chants of would-be beer drinkers at a baseball game, he had even less luck in the press. One of his chief tormentors was H. L. Mencken, the Baltimore-based columnist known for his zingers. Mencken (who frequently referred to Hoover as "Lord Herbert," or even more mean-spiritedly "Fat Herbert") was against Hoover from the start and would not concede that Hoover's embrace of Prohibition came about for any reason other than political convenience. As Mencken wrote, just prior to the 1928 election:

> Certainly no one who knows him believes that he is a Prohibitionist. He is simply a candidate for office, willing and eager to do or say anything that will get him votes, and the fortunes of war have made it more prudent for him to cultivate the drys than to cultivate the wets.

And then Mencken took Hoover to the woodshed for his see-no-evil existence in the Harding administration.

A HOOVER CLASSIC

While convalescing in a hospital in the Florida Keys, Hoover famously asked the Catholic hospital's main administrator Mother Magdalena if she could make a good dry martini. She duly complied. And while some may say the only good dry martini is one where the gin is stirred with ice and the word "vermouth" is merely uttered, below is a traditional recipe for the classic version.

Dry Martini

3 oz. gin
½ oz. vermouth, such as Vya Dry Vermouth
1 green cocktail olive for garnish

Combine the gin and the vermouth in a mixing glass two-thirds full of ice cubes and stir well. Strain into a chilled cocktail glass and add the garnish. (Alternatively, a lemon twist can be employed instead of the olive. But not a cocktail onion—that would make it a Gibson and not a martini.)

> He [Hoover] came from London, the wettest town in
> the world, to sit on the Harding cabinet, the wettest
> since the days of Noah. No one ever heard him utter
> a whisper against the guzzling that surrounded him.
> He was as silent about it as he was about the stealing.

Although typically wary of all politicians, Mencken backed Hoover's Democratic opponent Al Smith of New York City, a "wet" candidate if ever there was one. (When Prohibition was repealed, Budweiser sent the Budweiser wagon to Gotham to provide Smith with a ceremonial taste of the suds.) But Hoover trounced Smith in the election, and, given the Wall Street crash looming in the future, it may have been Al's lucky day when he lost.

HERBERT'S MAIN BEEF

Long before he became president, Hoover sided with the "dry" side, whether for political convenience, as Mencken suggested, or not. According to Hoover, it was to save every bit of wheat and barley to support both the Allied war effort in Europe or to feed the innocent civilians who inadvertently found themselves displaced and hungry during the horrific and widespread hostilities. "If I were dictator in this war I should stop brewing and distilling for beverage purposes at once," proclaimed Hoover, quoted in the *Saturday Evening Post* in 1917. "The product adds little or nothing to human nutrition—at best, it is a luxury."

Hoover himself, however, had not given up drinking at the time of his emphatic statement.

JUNIOR GETS A "PEP TALK"

When Herbert Hoover Jr. was selected to serve in John Foster Dulles's State Department during Eisenhower's presidency, he received perhaps some surprising advice from his aging father.

According to Richard Norton Smith's in-depth biography *An Uncommon Man: The Triumph of Herbert Hoover*, the ex-president told his junior namesake: "Herbert, keep a bottle of whiskey in your bottom drawer and after the day is over, when you're tired and before you start home, take a swig…and it will pep you up."

A MARTINI WITH MOTHER MAGDALENA

Hoover enjoyed relaxing and fishing in the Florida Keys during cold weather months. He picked up a case of pneumonia in March 1953, probably after attending the Eisenhower inauguration in Washington, D.C. But Hoover—almost eighty years of age at the time—stubbornly refused to seek medical attention and went down to Key Largo to fish.

But in Key Largo, Hoover's condition seemed to get worse and the ex-president was carted off by ambulance to a nearby Catholic hospital. When Hoover was checked in, he was visited by the hospital supervisor, Mother Magdalena, whereupon the one-time Wonder Boy must have caused some wonder when he cheekily inquired: "Sister, can you make a good dry martini?" But apparently without missing a beat, Mother Magdalena assured Hoover that she could indeed make a good dry martini—and then she proved it.

Sister, can you make a good dry martini?

BELGIUM RELIEF

According to at least one Prohibition historian, Hoover's drink with Mother Magdalena was far from his first dry martini. In his book *Last Call*, author Daniel Okrent records that Hoover—while a cabinet member for both President Harding and President Coolidge—would swing by the Embassy of Belgium (where he was technically not on U.S. soil) for a martini.

Having successfully headed up the Belgian Relief Fund (based out of London, where Hoover lived for a number of years) in

1914, he could count on a warm welcome, and apparently a cold libation of choice, at the Belgium Embassy.

As Hoover aptly put it later in life, a stiff cocktail could provide "the pause between the errors and trials of the day and the hopes of the night."

LAST CALL

Hoover grew up in West Branch, Iowa. He was raised as a Quaker and a Republican, recalling that one of the few Democrats in town was a notorious drunk.

Hoover had a stormy relationship with Congress and once referred to it as "that beer garden on the hill."

There's a bar in Seattle named "Hooverville," and its ambience on Yelp is described as "divey."

DWIGHT D.

EISENHOWER

★ 1953–1961 ★

"I SUPPOSE THIS CALLS FOR CHAMPAGNE."

—Dwight D. Eisenhower

LIKE RUNNING AGAINST WASHINGTON

"**T**HE MAN ON HORSEBACK"—a successful military
hero—has often been an unstoppable force in presidential races. Victorious generals, such as Andrew
Jackson, Zachary Taylor, and U. S. Grant, often hold a
competitive edge over less-decorated candidates.

So it was with Dwight D. "Ike" Eisenhower, the thir-
ty-fourth president of the United States. Riding a wave of
national adoration, Eisenhower—running on the Republican ticket—hammered the opposition in both the 1952
and 1956 elections. Unlike, say, the egotistical General
Douglas MacArthur, Ike also knew how to play the "Aw,
shucks, folks" card. As Democratic foe Adlai Stevenson (a
skilled and intelligent orator but twice trounced by Ike) put
it: "It was like running against George Washington."

Like Washington, Eisenhower enjoyed modest amounts
of alcohol, typically in social situations. Except for a few
wild moments in his early years, Ike rarely over-imbibed.
In fact, if Eisenhower could be said to have had one truly
bad habit, it was smoking. Against regulations, Ike began
rolling and smoking his own cigarettes at West Point. He
was said to have smoked several packs of Camels per day
during World War II. Although he allegedly went "cold
turkey" after the war, it is highly likely that Ike's poor health
(he had several heart attacks late in life, including one that
led to his death in 1968) had much to do with years of hard
smoking.

IRASCIBLE IKE?

The picture of unflappable General Eisenhower, coolly direct-ing the Normandy invasion and other critical campaigns of World War II, is a famous one. But those unfamiliar with the details of Dwight D. Eisenhower's young adulthood might find it hard to believe that in a fit of temper a whiskey-fueled Ike once put his fist through a wall. The incident occurred in the months after Ike's graduation from West Point, where Eisenhower had excelled on the football field. He suffered a career-ending injury in a game versus Tufts in 1913, but Ike no doubt still carried back to Kansas some of the swagger of the gridiron.

As Eisenhower biographer Carlo D'Este detailed in his 2003 book *Eisenhower: A Soldier's Life*:

> With little else to do in Abilene... Eisenhower could be found hunting, fishing, and occasionally drinking and playing poker. One evening he and several friends had imbibed enough bootleg whiskey to become loud and boisterous when they ambled into a local café. Eisenhower attempted to teach his friends some of his West Point songs in his dreadful singing voice.... Eisenhower defied several profane requests from the owner to stop or be tossed out, responding by angrily daring him to try; then, to make a point, he thrust his fist through the wall... where it became stuck. A portion of the wall had to be cut away with a kitchen knife to free a very chagrined Dwight Eisenhower.

In his later years, the five-star general and president claimed that the fist-in-the-wall incident had been dramatically embellished.

BATHTUB GIN

After World War I, Eisenhower and another West Point product, George Smith Patton, were stationed together at Fort Meade, Maryland. With Prohibition in full swing, the young officers and friends had no qualms about making their own alcohol. Patton bottled some of his homebrewed beer. But at least one account has it that the man who would become a celebrated expert on tank warfare was reduced to a "duck and cover" response one day when some of the bottles suddenly blew their tops—the sound apparently mimicking some kind of weaponry. (Except for some good-natured ribbing from his young wife, Patton, who would one day earn the nickname "Blood and Guts," escaped the incident unscathed.)

Ike was in the game for stronger stuff, even if the production process was less hazardous. He used grain alcohol and a bathtub to mix up a reasonable facsimile for gin.

SPECIAL KAY

With World War II in full swing, Eisenhower arrived in London—a proud city still standing, but smoldering from the Luftwaffe's brutal blitzkrieg. It was here that the rising American general was assigned a British captain to drive him around: an attractive, Irish-born strawberry blonde by the name of Kay Summersby.

If you want to start an argument in a roomful of Eisenhower "scholars" simply ask: "Were Eisenhower and Kay Summersby wartime lovers?" The historical flak—not all necessarily facts—will fly. Diehard Eisenhower supporters (and especially family members) typically tiptoe around this subject as if it were a minefield or blatantly deny that it ever could have happened. As for Summersby, in 1973—terminally ill with cancer—she penned a book entitled *Past Forgetting: My Love Affair with Dwight D. Eisenhower.*

John Eisenhower, the president's son, weighed in with an open mind—and offered the possibility that alcohol might well have played a role in any of his father's indiscretions—if, in fact, there were lapses in the general's discipline. Quoted in a 1977 Associated Press story, John Eisenhower allowed:

> Nobody can bear witness that something did not happen. How can I go on the witness stand some

WHAT IKE LIKED

While Ike occasionally liked to imbibe, among his favored concoctions was the old standard, scotch and soda. It's perhaps fitting that Eisenhower's personality mirrors that of his drink—unpretentious, tasteful, not particularly flamboyant, but certainly gets the job done.

Scotch and Soda

3 oz. scotch whisky

5 oz. club soda

Fill a highball glass with ice cubes, add the scotch, then fill the remainder of the glass with club soda. Stir gently.

place and swear Dad didn't get a couple of drinks of scotch in him sometime and get affection?

What we do know is that Ike and his driver-assistant were quite close and drinking buddies to boot, almost from day one. When Summersby initially drove Ike and General Mark Clark around England in 1942, she wrote:

> It was warm and I was parched. Without thinking how outrageous I was being, I pulled up in Beaconsfield and said, "You absolutely must visit an English pub."
> It was a gin and tonic kind of day. As we sat there and sipped our drinks, the late-spring afternoon slipped into evening. The nightingales were singing. It was high time for the three truants to get back to London.

Since the English are renowned for their top-shelf gin, one must assume it was better than the bathtub batches that Ike once mixed up during Prohibition. And since a lunch with wine had preceded the British gin tonics, one can picture the "three truants" feeling rather happy upon their return to the embattled capital.

CHAMPAGNE SPARKLE

Legend has it that when the monk Dom Perignon accidently "discovered" champagne, he urged his fellow monks: "Come quick, brothers! I am drinking stars!" Eisenhower didn't drink stars, but on some special occasions he had them pinned to his uniform—and that called for champagne. When Ike was awarded a fourth general's star (he eventually achieved five stars) in February 1943 en route to his selection as supreme commander of Allied forces, he saw fit to break out the bubbly. The end of the war was far from in sight (in fact, the Allies were still attempting to oust Axis forces from North Africa), but to hear Summersby tell it, the occasion was a rare one of splendid respite from Eisenhower's ever-increasing responsibilities:

> That night Ike broke out the champagne and we had an impromptu party just for our headquarters group. He was very, very happy that evening. I'll never forget the sheer pleasure that radiated from him. I remember thinking, *There's a man who has never had very much fun in his life.* The General was always very charming, always had that grin at the ready, but underneath it all he was a very serious and lonely man who worried, worried, worried.

HOT DOGS AND BEER

Ike was serving as president of Columbia University in 1949 when he made a speech at an elite New York City hotel that rattled some members of working-class America and drew fire from the Columbia student body.

Eisenhower insinuated that perhaps some Americans harbored high-roller tastes for "caviar and champagne" when "hotdogs and beer" might be a more realistic fare for the masses. Even the student newspaper at Columbia did not let this comment slide without a well-aimed jab at the general:

... [A]ny citizen... may some day eat champagne and caviar, and in the White House at that.

> Being content with beer and hot dogs has never been a part of the American tradition we know. The one we know assures any citizen that he may some day eat champagne and caviar, and in the White House at that. We don't know, of course, but we are willing to bet that beer and hot dogs weren't on the menu at the Waldorf-Astoria last Wednesday night either.

A few days later, piqued students took it to the next level: they decorated Alexander Hamilton's statue at Columbia with an empty beer carton and a half dozen or so hot dogs and added five stars onto Hamilton's bronze derriere. The students also hung a protest sign around Hamilton's neck that read: "Ike prefers beer and franks for all." Controversy aside, one year later Eisenhower was a serious candidate for president of the United States.

SCOTCH-LIKING IKE

Eisenhower acquired a taste for scotch whisky during his military career, and he would occasionally indulge in a glass or two during his presidential years and in retirement. State dinners at the White House were accompanied by wine and champagne. But when President Eisenhower and the first lady entertained at their home in Gettysburg, it was standard procedure to serve cocktails—the American libation of choice in the 1950s. The Gettysburg home had all the cocktail-making equipment—ice buckets, shakers, shot glasses, and bar glasses—to concoct a potent highball.

Before their falling out, Ike sent a nice bottle of scotch to then president Harry Truman (who, as is well known, preferred bourbon whiskey but would, on occasion, settle for scotch) in 1946. Truman responded with a thank-you letter, reflecting both his sense of humor concerning alcohol and his obvious fondness for Ike. "I think I'll inhale it rather than pass it out to these 'thugs' who hang around here and drink my whiskey," joked the man from Missouri. "Maybe you and I could think up an occasion when we could share it."

But the Eisenhower-Truman relationship was destined to become as icy as any cocktail recipe that says the drink must be served "on the rocks."

FIXING THE FEUD

When Dwight D. Eisenhower aligned himself with the Republicans, Truman (who had wished to entice the popular general into the Democratic camp) and Ike began to drift apart.

Their relationship hit its lowest point after Eisenhower arrived at the White House on his 1953 Inauguration Day. Presidential protocol typically requires that the incoming president goes inside to be greeted by the outgoing one. But Eisenhower ignored this tradition and refused to leave the presidential limo. Eventually, a snubbed Truman was forced to come out to Ike and proceed to the inauguration ceremony in what must have been an awkward ride for all involved. (One can almost imagine the steam escaping from "Give 'Em Hell Harry's" ears and fogging up his trademark glasses.)

> They had a few drinks and, oh, talked about old times.

More than a decade passed before the two men—both ex-presidents by then—patched up their differences. Both were in Washington to attend John F. Kennedy's funeral, and a simple twist of fate (or perhaps some man's deliberate stroke of genius) happened to place Ike and Truman in the same limousine. As the *Washington Post*'s White House correspondent Edward Folliard noted:

> But at any rate, the limousine brought them back from Arlington on this sad day, and drew up at Blair House where Mr. Truman was staying... Well, as Truman got out of the limousine, he turned around, and said: "Ike, how about coming in for a drink?"
>
> And Ike looked at Mamie and she seemed to agree so they went in... and they had a few drinks and, oh, talked about old times, and finally when it was time to go, Mamie Eisenhower thanked Mr. Truman for something he had done just before the inauguration in 1953. Truman without consulting with Ike had arranged for John Eisenhower, their son, to be sent back from Korea. He

ordered him back for the inauguration. Mamie thanked him for that and then kissed him. That was the end of the feud, and they once again were the friends they had been for many years.

DR. SNYDER AND THE SECOND SCOTCH

Being Eisenhower's physician was not without its challenges, but Dr. Howard Snyder—a friend of Ike's to boot—did his best. By some accounts, Eisenhower had four heart attacks (the first coming during his first term) and more than a dozen incidents of cardiac arrest during his seventy-nine years of life.

Dr. Snyder was vehemently supportive of Ike's golf habit, noting that the president was "like a caged lion" if he did not get to play. He also managed to get Eisenhower to cut way down on his once-massive cigarette addiction.

But the former D-Day commander did not lose every battle. Snyder had tried to restrict Ike to a solitary glass of scotch and soda for his nightcap. When Ike asked the butler to bring him reinforcements, the doc reminded him: "I said only one, Mister President." And Ike would pleasantly reply: "Thank you, Howard. You've done your duty."

Then he would turn to the butler, smile, and firmly state: "Bring me a second scotch."

LAST CALL......................

Eisenhower probably would have chosen golf over booze; he haunted the links whenever possible during his presidential terms. Any alcohol would have waited until the last round had been completed.

NIXON

★ 1969 - 1974 ★

"LET US DRINK TO GENERATIONS TO COME WHO MAY
HAVE A BETTER CHANCE TO LIVE IN PEACE BECAUSE OF
WHAT WE HAVE DONE."

—Richard Nixon

KICKING AROUND NIXON

I N NOVEMBER 1962, Richard Nixon—having been soundly thrashed in the race for the California governorship—delivered one of his most famous lines. Insinuating that a predatory press was partly responsible for his defeat, Nixon quipped: "You won't have Nixon to kick around anymore, because, gentlemen, this is my last press conference...."

As fate would have it, Nixon was wrong on both counts. It was far from Nixon's last press conference, and, five decades later, Nixon continues to be "kicked around" by the press—if anything, with increased vigor. David Fulsom's 2012 book *Nixon's Darkest Secrets* is particularly brutal and includes a chapter titled: "The World's Most Powerful Drunk."

Alcohol certainly played a role in Nixon's worst moments—especially during the 1972 Watergate scandal and his eventual resignation in 1974 (he was the only president to resign from office). But Nixon also hoisted alcohol in triumph on rare occasions—such as his trip to China.

But with the stresses of being president in general and the added burden of Watergate in particular, it's no wonder that Nixon was drawn to drink. This, combined with the fact that he reached a state of intoxication quite rapidly, resulted in some very colorful anecdotes involving Richard M. Nixon and Demon Alcohol.

THIS WINE IS MINE

Nixon lived up to his nickname, "Tricky Dick," when serving wine at his White House dinners. The thirty-seventh president of the United States certainly knew and relished wines from the world's most renowned cellars. In fact, Nixon often had his wine glass filled with a fine French vintage, a 1957 Château Lafite Rothschild. His guests, however, were typically given a decent though far less expensive wine; the waiters were instructed to serve it with a towel wrapped around the bottle so as to hide the label.

In some circles, this sly practice—serving a mediocre brand of booze to others while saving the top-shelf stuff for oneself—has been dubbed "pulling a Nixon."

MAOTAI MOMENTS

From World War II on, virtually all U.S. presidents had to deal with either Russian vodka or the potent Chinese liquor called maotai at one point or another. Drinking these powerful alcohols "came with the territory," so to speak, because international protocol often mandated partaking in toasts even if they amounted to little more than token sips.

Richard Nixon drank vodka with the Russian leaders and, more famously, maotai with the Chinese. Maotai is an extremely potent alcohol, typically about 110 proof, distilled from sorghum. Journalist Dan Rather—with maybe only slight exaggeration—once compared the consumption of this traditional Chinese libation to "drinking liquid razor blades."

Perhaps the major triumph of the Nixon White House occurred in February 1972 when the administration visited the People's Republic of China. One of the strategic goals of this historic tour was to keep the Soviets "honest" by, at least in appearance, cozying up to the Chinese. As Nixon's secretary of state Dr. Henry Kissinger tellingly put it, the U.S. might be able to "have its Russian vodka and its maotai, too." (In less cryptic language,

Kissinger allowed that a friendly visit to China might establish more "equilibrium" in the world.)

Knowing that there was bound to be some toasting between U.S. officials and their Chinese counterparts, Chief of Staff General Alexander Haig sent forth a cable warning against the mind-numbing properties of the infamous maotai. (Haig knew of what he spoke: he had jousted with the formidable liquid on an advance trip to the Chinese capital just the month before.) Haig's memo all but came with a blinking red light and beeping warning signal, no doubt taking into account that Nixon was a notorious lightweight when it came to handling much more modest alcohols than the legendary maotai.

Haig's cable read: "UNDER NO... REPEAT... NO CIRCUMSTANCES SHOULD THE PRESIDENT ACTUALLY DRINK FROM HIS GLASS IN RESPONSE TO BANQUET TOAST."

Nixon rose to the occasion. After toasts with Chinese premier Chou En-lai, the president approached each table and (taking small sips!) toasted all of the important banquet participants. Somewhat surprisingly, the chief executive managed to stay apparently sober throughout the festivities.

As a bonus, Chou En-lai playfully demonstrated just how powerful maotai could be. Putting a match to a cup of the volatile liquid, he announced: "Mr. Nixon, please take a look. It can indeed catch fire!"

BURNING DOWN THE HOUSE

The band Talking Heads formed just about the same time Nixon was drummed out of the White House. But perhaps the band's hit 1980s song "Burning Down the House" conjured up a smile years later among those privy to one particular Nixon episode.

The story, once again, involves maotai. According to some accounts, Nixon attempted to duplicate Chou En-lai's fiery demonstration at the Peking banquet, only this time in the White House dining room.

Henry Kissinger recounted the incident—perhaps somewhat embellished—in a welcoming toast to Vice Premier Deng

MIXIN' A NIXON

Belfast-born Joe Gilmore, the highly touted and creative mix-
ologist at the American Bar in London's Savoy Hotel, made
many a cocktail in honor of celebrities. In 1969, Nixon was
coming off his 1968 election victory over Hubert Humphrey
and third-party "Deep South" candidate George Wallace.
Watergate was far in the future, and Nixon was riding high.
So, in honor of the president's 1969 visit to Britain, Gilmore
whipped up this concoction dubbed:

> **The Nixon**
> 1 part bourbon whiskey
> 1 part sloe gin
> 2 dashes of peach bitters
>
> *Stir and then serve "on the rocks."*

Perhaps following the "If Mohammed won't come to the
mountain, move the mountain to Mohammed" theory, Gilmore mixed the drink at the American Bar but then sent it over
to the Claridge Hotel, where the president and his entourage
were staying. There is no proof that Nixon actually drank "The
Nixon," but how many people can claim that the famous
bartender Gilmore created a drink in their honor?

Xiaoping when the Chinese leader visited the United States on April 14, 1974. The toast was offered at a dinner held at New York City's swanky Waldorf-Astoria and unfolded like this:

> Henry Kissinger: I think if we drink enough maotai we can solve anything.
>
> Deng Xiaoping: Then when I go back to China, I must increase production of it.
>
> HK: You know, when the President came back from China, he wanted to show his daughter how potent maotai was. So he took out a bottle and poured it into a saucer and lit it, but the glass bowl broke and the maotai ran over the table and the table began to burn! So you nearly burned down the White House!

Kissinger then lifted his glass to all the guests and they drank to Nixon's alleged mishap.

DRUNK DIALING

If the tale of Nixon and an almost-flaming White House was a little exaggerated, the fact that his administration was about to implode was not; the Watergate scandal was about to take down Nixon and many of his top men. As federal investigators began to close in, the president weirdly indulged in some "drunk-dialing" incidents.

Nixon's slurred speech is quite apparent on the Watergate-era tapes. But the president's strange actions are also well documented by some of his trusted inner circle—including John Ehrlichman (domestic council chief), who witnessed an intoxicated Nixon's late-night rambling over the phone lines. Apparently, the beleaguered president stooped to such actions in an attempt to measure the loyalty of others or to have them understand the weight of his Watergate woes.

One frequent late night target was the lawyer Leonard Garment, who served as White House counsel and as a special consultant on various projects. Concerning Nixon's late night phone calls, Ehrlichman recalled:

> He (Nixon) would talk to political people. Then for the last call, he'd say: "Get me Len." By that time we would have given him his Seconal (a sleeping pill) and a good stiff single malt scotch. And he'd get on the phone with [Garment] until the phone dropped from his fingers and he fell asleep. Then I'd pick up the phone very quietly, and hang up.

LONDON CALLING

If Nixon was guilty of sometimes phoning others while under the influence, on at least one important occasion he also was incapacitated to an extent that he wasn't able to field an important call from British prime minister Edward Heath.

On October 11, 1973, Heath attempted to contact Nixon to discuss the outbreak of hostilities between Israel and the Arabs, but the talk had to be postponed. When Brent Scowcroft (Kissinger's assistant) called to alert the White House that Heath was eager to discuss the situation, a hesitant Kissinger replied: "Can we tell them no? When I talked to the president, he was loaded."

Did Scowcroft answer: "What! The president's loaded?!"?

No, he did not.

Seemingly unsurprised, Scowcroft, rather nonchalantly, answered: "Right. OK. I will say the president won't be available until the first thing in the morning...."

> When I talked to the president, he was loaded.

THE CHINA TOAST

Not all of Nixon's drinking stories are negative ones. After successfully reestablishing ties with China and gaining the go-ahead to visit that country with an official message from Chou En-lai, Nixon was understandably quite jubilant, and he toasted Henry Kissinger in the Lincoln Sitting Room at the White House. Nixon proudly included this anecdote in his memoirs:

> In one of the cabinets I found an unopened bottle of very old Courvosier [sic] brandy that someone had given us for Christmas. I tucked it under my arm and took two large snifters from the glass cupboard. As we raised our glasses, I said: "Henry, we are drinking a toast not to ourselves personally or to our success, or to our administration's policies which have made this message and made tonight possible. Let us drink to generations to come who may have a better chance to live in peace because of what we have done."

As it turned out, some three years later, the same bottle of brandy was called upon. Nixon asked Kissinger to have a drink with him and then to join him in prayer on a dramatically more somber occasion: Richard Milhous Nixon's resignation.

THE CHINA (SLOSHED) SYNDROME

While Nixon was relatively well behaved at official banquets during the China visit, he apparently went over the edge at a plush high-rise hotel in Shanghai on his last night in the country. As the historian Robert Dalleck related in a 2007 interview with PBS (discussing his book, *Partners in Power: Nixon and Kissinger*):

> Nixon was drinking all afternoon, Mao-ties, and he was pretty well sloshed.... At 2:00 in the morning, he called [Bob] Haldeman and Kissinger to his suite and he almost begs them to assure him that this is

going to be a great success, that the press isn't going
to blight this achievement.

The press, for the most part, applauded Nixon's diplomatic trip
to China. But the Watergate break-in was just a few months away,
and Nixon's finest hour was fading fast.

THE ELUSIVE DR. K

It is difficult to pin down exactly how the brilliant Dr. Henry
Kissinger (named Nixon's security advisor in 1969 and his secretary of state in 1973) felt about Nixon and, for that matter, the
extent of Nixon's drinking.

Kissinger is on the record as saying stories of Nixon drinking
himself into a useless stupor were "absurd." But he also notes that
two glasses of wine might result in Nixon slurring his words or
becoming either overly sentimental or, conversely, combative or
vulgar. In fact, behind the president's back, Kissinger sometimes
referred to Nixon as "our drunken friend" to other staff members.

Then again, Nixon was not always polite to Kissinger. He sometimes made snide remarks in front of Kissinger and behind his
back to others.

GOOD QUESTION

Just ten months after his resignation, Nixon was brought before
a grand jury and made to listen to a slew of tapes from the Watergate
days. On more than a couple of tapes, it is quite obvious that
Nixon was slurring his words. To which the former president could
not help muttering: "I wonder what I had to drink that day?"

A good question indeed! (And "how much"?) Like James
Buchanan, Nixon liked many different kinds of alcohol, though he
was very much lacking in "Old Buck's" tolerance. Nixon certainly
drank various rum concoctions (particularly when he hobnobbed
with tycoon Bebe Rebozo in Florida), top-shelf wines and cham-
pagnes, dry martinis, vodka, scotch, brandy, and, of course, the
famous Chinese maotai.

LAST CALL

Richard Nixon may have displayed alcohol issues as early as 1959. On a trip to Moscow for the so-called "Kitchen Debates," then vice president Nixon reportedly downed half a dozen vodka martinis and uttered some vulgarities.

A California Angels fan, Nixon was invited into the clubhouse after that team won its first divisional playoff title in 1979. The Angels were in the full flight of festivities when second baseman Bobby Grich famously poured a full beer on the former president's head.

GERALD

FORD

★ 1974–1977 ★

"THE THREE-MARTINI LUNCH IS THE EPITOME
OF AMERICAN EFFICIENCY."

—Gerald Ford

THE DRINKS GO WITH THE JOB

GERALD "JERRY" FORD was dealt less than an ideal hand when he was called upon by bizarre circumstances to replace a disgraced Spiro Agnew as vice president and then to finish out Nixon's disastrous shortened term after Watergate. Some felt Ford wasn't intelligent enough to be the thirty-eighth president of the United States. Lyndon Johnson claimed—with typical mean-spiritedness—that Ford must have played too much football without a helmet. But perhaps a modest mind is precisely what those troubled times called for.

Born Leslie King Jr., the future president changed to his stepfather's name of Ford when he was still a boy. His biological father was an alcoholic who physically abused Ford's mother—the primary reason she divorced King and remarried.

Like most U.S. congressmen, Jerry Ford found daily drinks just part of the Washington terrain—no big deal. When he stepped up to the White House after Nixon's resignation, however, Ford suddenly needed to downshift to a slightly less liquid routine—a change that took longer than expected and was not without a few amusing miscues.

First lady Betty Ford had serious issues with alcohol and drug abuse; but by most accounts she is given high marks for not only facing up to her own demons and conversing candidly about them, but also helping others in similar predicaments through the renowned efforts of the Betty Ford Center.

THE MIGHTY MARTINI

Jerry Ford was a tenacious football letter–winner at Michigan in the 1930s and helped take the Wolverines to two national titles. In an era when the best athletes on the field still played "both ways," Ford starred at center and also performed as linebacker. He knocked heads with some of the best collegiate players of his era.

Ford the politician, however, had trouble holding his own when he went head-to-head with the small-but-mighty martini. As he was already accused of being clumsy (his occasional tumbles drew attention from Saturday Night Live, providing ample fodder for comedian Chevy Chase), his fondness for these tongue-tying concoctions did nothing to dispel accusations that Ford was less than articulate. But to give Ford the benefit of the doubt, there is no proof that his clumsy incidents were alcohol-related—though both he and the first lady drank routinely on Air Force One, and some of his untimely trips did occur while getting on and off the aircraft.

On at least one occasion, however, alcohol was identified as the culprit behind a less-than-stellar speech. As veteran journalist Bob Woodward chronicled in *Shadow: Five Presidents and the Legacy of Watergate*.

> Ford was unaccustomed to the high level of scrutiny. He was used to the Congressional lifestyle, which often included alcohol at lunch. This habit proved particularly embarrassing for Ford when he gave a luncheon speech. Once, in Denver, he skipped several dozen pages of his remarks because he had what his aides called a few "marts" (for martinis), before speaking.

WHAT'S UP, DOC?

To diffuse the ongoing issue of the martini in the chief executive's daily routine, William Lukash—the White House physician and a navy admiral—confronted Ford with some blunt advice. In

Woodward's account, Lukash firmly stated: "You're President of the United States. Stop drinking. Especially stop drinking martinis at lunch."

Ford had his own special "humor writer," a man by the name of Don Penny. Penny's job was to help Ford weave some jokes into his speeches, but he, too, felt the president's fondness for a martini or two at midday was no laughing matter. After Ford mispronounced some words in a speech, Penny—after confirming that martinis were part of the problem—also approached Ford about it.

Ford eventually heard from enough advisors, got the message, and cut back on his lunchtime libations. But it did not stop Ford from vigorously defending that fine drink when President Carter later tried to tax the well-entrenched "three-martini lunch."

PARDONS AND PEANUTS

Can anyone blame Jerry Ford if he downed a few stiff ones before (and after) he made the decision to pardon Richard Milhous Nixon? Ford called the controversial pardon "the end of our national nightmare," but there are those who also believe it seriously hurt his election chances against Jimmy Carter in 1976. Certainly ultraconservative Joseph Coors—owner of the esteemed Coors brewery in Colorado—thought so, and put his support and money behind Ronald Reagan, albeit unsuccessfully, in the Republican primaries. The Democrats made the Nixon pardon part of their attack plan, of course, and Jimmy Carter prevailed.

Martinis, once again, emerged as a gremlin in the Ford campaign. Ford—trying to suggest that Carter would diminish America's military might—liked to riff off the famous and much-quoted Teddy Roosevelt catchphrase of "Speak softly, and carry a big stick." He would then follow TR's line with: "Jimmy Carter says, 'Speak softly, and carry a flyswatter....'" But as Thomas DeFrank (a Ford aide and eventual biographer) noted in his book *Write It When I'm Gone*:

> At one torchlight rally at the end of a long day and after a couple of martinis, it took Ford three times to

BUBBLY AND BLUE

Jerry Ford is perhaps better known for his wife's drinking than his own. (Betty Ford bravely overcame alcohol and drug addiction and went on to found the Betty Ford Center, for the treatment of alcoholism and other chemical dependency.) But Ford did enjoy his martinis, and the Ford White House also celebrated—or commiserated—their last days in office with cocktails. When the liquor was depleted, they resorted to champagne. In a nod to those last days in office, and to Ford's collegiate football career with the University of Michigan, here is the Go Blue! Champagne Cocktail.

Go Blue! Champagne Cocktail

½ oz. Blue Curacao liqueur
½ oz. orange flavored vodka
3–4 oz. chilled champagne

Pour liqueur and vodka into a cocktail shaker half-filled with ice. Strain into a chilled champagne flute, top with champagne, and serve.

nail the punch line: "Speak softly, and carry a fly-washer... flyspotter... flyswatter."

MISTER PEANUT PREVAILS

Ford—former star athlete and congressional heavyweight—had trouble accepting that the American people had chosen the former peanut farmer over him. (According to one story, a frustrated Ford once blurted out that Carter was an "S.O.B.") Along the same lines, Ford's outgoing staff, having served less than three years in the White House, also proved to be less than good sports. The fact that some of Carter's advance staffers began to move into the White House early rubbed salt in the wound.

> ...We drank all the liquor we could find.

Ford had lost, and his staffers were out of a job in arguably the most important city in the world. As Ford's press secretary Ron Nessen later admitted:

> On Ford's last night in the White House, I and my press office staff, all feeling sad, gave ourselves a farewell party. First we downed several bottles of champagne purchased for the occasion. When that was gone, we drank all the liquor we could find in cabinets and closets. And when that was gone, we even consumed an old bottle of fizzy white wine brought home from a Ford visit to Romania. We dimmed the lights to match our mood.

When some members of the Ford team (including the former president and Betty) left the White House for California the next day, it was said that everyone onboard a backup plane (Carter did not grant permission for them to use Air Force One) refused to eat the peanuts from an offering of mixed nuts. Then, in a fit of political pique (reinforced, perhaps by semi-serious hangovers), they purposely tossed the peanuts around the aircraft.

DON'T SHOOT ME, I'M ONLY JERRY FORD

Gerald Ford managed to survive two assassination attempts (both by women), despite serving less than a full term in the White House. The first bungled attempt was by Charles Manson devotee Lynnette "Squeaky" Fromme in Sacramento on September 5, 1975 (she failed to have a bullet in the firing chamber). A few weeks later, as Ford left the St. Francis Hotel in San Francisco, Sara Jane Moore took an unsuccessful pop at the president (she accidently winged a cab driver). After Moore was subdued, the Secret Service rushed Ford to the airport, onto Air Force One, and roared off to the presumed safety of Washington.

> The booze and black humor flowed.

Having been off doing her own thing during the day and not having heard any radio reports, Betty Ford innocently asked her husband something like: "How did your day go, dear?"

According to Nessen: "I think it was [Secretary of State Donald] Rumsfeld who finally told her that someone took a shot at the president.... We took off and what had happened sunk in. I can tell you quite a few martinis were consumed on the flight back."

In addition, Nessen observed: "The booze and black humor flowed. Someone asked if legislation granting equal rights to women included equal rights to take a shot at the President...."

Supporting Nessen's scenario, Kenneth T. Walsh wrote in his book *Air Force One*:

> More than anything, there was the consumption of a considerable amount of alcohol, to the point where

some staffers got tipsy. Ford had a couple of martinis, extra dry, and Mrs. Ford had vodka tonic on ice, as everyone tried to relax and count their blessings.

Ford, apparently, was far less shaken than his martinis. He rather casually phoned his children to let them know he was fine. In addition to his post–assassination attempt libations, the former gridiron star wolfed down a sizeable beefsteak before nodding off to sleep.

Ford lived to ninety-three—still a presidential record. He died in December 2006.

BETTY FORD: TRIALS AND TRIBULATIONS

Betty Ford certainly was not the only first lady with substance abuse problems, but she was probably the most forthright in later acknowledging them. (Mrs. Ford was similarly open about her mastectomy for breast cancer.)

Betty Ford began problem drinking while her husband was away in Washington during his days in Congress. Her drinking became even more problematic and was accelerated by an addiction to painkillers that occurred after she pinched a nerve in her neck. Attempts at moderation did not work. As Betty noted: "Jerry would hand me a mild vodka and tonic and I'd sigh, 'Why don't you give me a normal drink?'"

Betty Ford's addiction to painkillers and alcohol seemingly increased after the former president and she moved back to California, eventually settling in Rancho Mirage in 1977. On April Fools' Day, 1978, the family (including Jerry Ford) confronted Betty in an "intervention," with daughter Susan Ford spearheading the effort. "I saw a very sluggish person," Susan later remarked in a PBS special. "It was like watching a robot in slow motion."

After initial tears and anger (Betty accused her family of being unfeeling "monsters") of denial, the intervention resulted in the former first lady checking into the Long Beach Naval Hospital in California. Betty's experience there planted the seeds for establishing what would become the Betty Ford Center—a detox program known for attracting famous clientele, such as Liz Taylor, Liza Minnelli, baseball stars Darryl Strawberry and Dwight Gooden, and—more recently—Lindsay Lohan.

Once she confronted her addiction, Ford spoke bluntly about the power it held over her. "I liked alcohol," she wrote in 1987. "It made me feel warm. And I loved pills. They took away my tension and pain."

Her announcement gave others the courage to be open about their substance abuse issues, too. The public and most of her friends were sympathetic to her struggle and complimentary of her courageous response to her problems. When Elizabeth "Betty" Ford died in July 2011, the *New York Times* obituary stated: "Few first ladies have been as popular as Betty Ford, and it was her frankness and lack of pretense that made her so."

TABLE DANCER

If there is one signature photograph from the presidential years that best reflects Betty Ford's free-spiritedness, that photo is arguably David Hume Kennerly's classic of the first lady dancing barefoot on the White House table. There were some initial concerns that some people—given Betty's history—might assume she'd been intoxicated at the time. But apparently the first lady was simply feeling impish and wanted to punctuate her departure from the White House with a bit of unpretentious fun.

LAST CALL

Presidential son Jack Ford apparently liked to have some fun, too. He invited Bianca Jagger—then wife of Mick, of Rolling Stones fame—to the White House for a drink. Allegedly it led to some kind of romantic encounter, possibly referred to in the Stones's song "Respectable."

RONALD

REAGAN

★ 1981–1989 ★

"I ENJOY A COCKTAIL NOW AND THEN BEFORE DINNER
AND HAVE A TASTE FOR A GOOD DINNER WINE."

—Ronald Reagan

A CONSERVATIVE DRINKER

RONALD REAGAN is regarded as a founding father of modern conservatism. But Republicans aren't the only ones who unabashedly wax nostalgic for the Reagan days; many Democrats quote him, as if to preemptively steal the Reagan rhetorical thunder.

Regardless of how you view the Reagan era, his election record shows that he hammered Carter in 1980 (taking forty-four states) and obliterated Walter Mondale in an even larger landslide in 1984. When he left office, Reagan had the loftiest approval rating of any president since FDR. The fortieth president also had a sense of humor and deployed it often, no matter how dire the moment might have appeared. When he was wheeled into the hospital after an assassin's bullet collapsed his lung on March 30, 1981, he managed to quip to the medical personnel: "I hope you're all Republicans!"

The future president grew up with some family dysfunction: his father, Jack Reagan, was an alcoholic. So the son never underestimated the damage that alcohol was capable of inflicting. That traumatic experience helped Ronald Reagan form his moderate drinking habits.

Still, Reagan liked a good glass of red and was skilled at the witty art of giving toasts—even to long-time political enemies like Tip O'Neill. And Reagan certainly wasn't above sampling an Irish lager on St. Paddy's Day.

THE GHOSTBUSTER BLUSH

Michael K. Deaver, one of Ronald Reagan's most trusted advisors, expertly staged some of the president's "photo ops" (for instance, on the D-Day beaches of Normandy for the fortieth anniversary of that battle, atop the Great Wall of China, and loading up sandbags in flood-ravaged Mississippi, for example). Deaver helped his boss "look good" for public-speaking engagements.

Despite his Hollywood background (or perhaps because of it), Reagan resisted any attempts to get him into a makeup room prior to appearances. But Deaver learned early on that there was one trick that gave Reagan a bit of color in his otherwise ghostly pale face: a glass of red wine. "Well, he could not resist a good French wine, and I figured if I put the bottle on the table, and he could see the vintage and the label, he'd have to have a taste," Deaver recalled in 2004. "And of course it brought all the capillaries out in his cheek.... and it worked."

> Well, he could not resist a good French wine....

Both California guys, Reagan and Deaver knew a lot about the best U.S. vintages, too. So even for simple cosmetic purposes, the president never drank mediocre wine—be those vintages from France or the so-called "Left Coast."

SINS OF THE FATHER

Jack Reagan, the future president's father and a man who barely subsisted during the Great Depression by selling shoes, suffered from alcoholism. Despite the trauma of these childhood experiences, Reagan often said he loved his father and learned some life lessons from him—beyond the obvious one of alcohol's potential for destruction. Reagan's mother Nelle told her sons that their father's inability to handle drinking was "a sickness."

THE SODA POP LESSON

Young Ronald—on one memorable occasion—obtained some firsthand knowledge on the subject of alcohol when he downed too much liquor during his student days at Eureka College. Claiming "curiosity" led him to over-imbibe with a couple of more experienced fraternity brothers, Reagan confessed in his autobiography: "It was during Prohibition and a lot of movies depicted illicit drinking as 'collegiate'... I'd take a big drink, as if it was a bottle of soda pop...."

The result, if not pretty (Reagan described himself as "blind drunk") provided an indelible lesson.

> ...they brought me back to the frat house and threw me in a shower. They had to smuggle me in, because everyone was in bed asleep. I woke up the next day with a terrible hangover. That was it for me. Although in later years I might have a cocktail before dinner, or a glass of wine with dinner, I'd been taught a lesson. I decided if that's what you get for drinking—a sense of helplessness—I didn't want any part of it.

HAVE PUB, WILL TRAVEL

Like most U.S. presidents with roots "across the pond," Ronald Reagan made it a point to visit the village of his Irish ancestors (in Ballyporeen, County Tipperary) when he traveled to the Emerald Isle in June 1984. The traveling party spent the first night at the lavish Ashford Castle in Galway. Reagan and his wife, Nancy—jet-lagged from the flight—turned in early. But the staffs—both visiting Yanks and hosting Irish—turned aggressively festive.

As one recollection, printed in the *Irish Voice* decades later, put it:

It was the night that Secretary of State George Shultz sang "Galway Bay" and Michael Deaver, special assistant to the president, sang "Danny Boy." Then Irish Minister for Foreign Affairs Peter Barry sang, as befitting a Cork man, "The Banks of My Own Lovely Lee," and then Secretary of the Department of Foreign Affairs Sean Donlon manned the piano all evening. It got so loud that they were warned they might wake the president up.

President Reagan and Nancy slept through all this moonlit malarkey. The most committed revelers, in fact, partied until the sunrise splashed some sense on the survivors, though as Irish-American journalist Niall O'Dowd unflinchingly put it: "There were certainly many sore heads on both sides the next morning."

THE RONALD REAGAN LOUNGE

Once in the village of Ballyporeen, Reagan received a few gifts from the locals and spoke briefly to them. This was after he had visited O'Farrell's, the local pub—later renamed "The Ronald Reagan Lounge." Reagan barely sampled a pint of Guinness in the pub (then switched to Smithwicks, which he also did not finish) and then only after Secret Service agents had sampled the mug first.

When the Ronald Reagan Lounge/O'Farrell's closed in 2004, the wooden bar and most of the establishment's barroom paraphernalia were purchased by the Reagan Library and Museum, shipped to Simi Valley, California, and given a new home in an old aircraft hanger—alongside Air Force One.

THE PUB PHOTO OP

The Reagan team realized early on that an occasional photo of their man hoisting a brew with the average guy in a pub helped balance out any "fat cat" accusations. Never mind that the president rarely swallowed more than a few swigs.

> Reagan... had
> a few sips of beer...
> and dined on
> traditional corned
> beef and cabbage.

In January 1983, Reagan was on a routine tour of some tech facilities in Boston when his entourage took a detour for a late lunch at the Eire Pub in blue-collar Dorchester. Apparently, two of Reagan's Secret Service agents were from the area and knew the pub well. Political cynics said the stop may have been, in part, to counterbalance a recent TV appearance at the fictional *Cheers* bar by Democratic heavyweight House Speaker Thomas "Tip" O'Neill—in essence, to show that President Reagan was capable of hoisting a brew with working-class men, in real time.

Similarly, revelers at Pat Troy's Ireland's Own pub in Alexandria, Virginia, were astounded to see Ronald Reagan saunter through the doors on St. Patrick's Day 1988. (Some of the president's advance men had been there before and thoroughly scouted out the tavern.) Reagan, accompanied by journalist James Kilpatrick, had a few sips of beer (Harp, an Irish lager, Troy later said) and dined on traditional corned beef and cabbage. Troy robustly led his loyal patrons in the various enactments of the "Unicorn Song"—a St. Paddy's Day ritual (typically booze-propelled) that the amused president apparently had not previously witnessed. Now retired from the bar business, the Irish-born Troy often describes the Reagan appearance as "awesome."

RUSSIANS AND VODKA

Like most American leaders from FDR on, President Reagan had to deal with the Russians, which meant vodka would always be close at hand for any summit meetings—even though Soviet president Mikhail Gorbachev, during Reagan's time, was futilely attempting to wean his countrymen from the clear-but-powerful elixir.

THE ORANGE BLOSSOM SPECIAL

If the president was not a big beer drinker, he did occasionally indulge in an Orange Blossom, which typically consists of:

> 1 oz. (or slightly less in Reagan's case) vodka
> 1 oz. of either grenadine or sweet vermouth
> 2 oz. fresh orange juice
>
> *Bring all ingredients together in a barroom glass filled with ice.*

Though Orange Blossoms often are made with gin, Reagan would have substituted vodka because, by some accounts, he did not react well to gin (he perhaps had an allergy to it). President Reagan also enjoyed an occasional screwdriver (vodka and orange juice).

Although the Russians were trying to downshift on vodka consumption back at home, they had no problem downing bottles of booze abroad. As Secretary of State George P. Shultz noted:

> At the first day's session at the Soviet embassy, nice motherly Russian ladies pushed vodka on our security people and pushed it hard. The Americans all declined, but the Russians partook enthusiastically. In the afternoon session at the American mission, bottles of Jack Daniel's and Johnnie Walker Black Label had been set on a table outside the meeting room; Soviet security guards drained them all.

No doubt President Reagan was pleased by this steadfast show of American restraint in the face of Russian temptation.

TWENTY-ONE:
IT'S NOT JUST FOR BLACKJACK ANYMORE

If you are nineteen or twenty and disappointed that you cannot sip a legal drink in the USA, then you might want to wing darts at Reagan's portrait. Reagan pushed hard to obtain an across-the-nation uniform age—twenty-one—for the legal consumption of alcohol.

The stats suggest that raising the drinking age to twenty-one saved lives. Reagan's comments and letters absolutely reflect his sincerity on the controversial issue. "We know that drinking plus driving spell death and disaster," Reagan said upon signing the National Minimum Drinking Age Act on July 17, 1984. "We know that people in the 18–20 age group are more likely to be in alcohol-related accidents...."

GREAT SCOTT!
DEBATING REAGAN ON THE DRINKING AGE

About six months after Reagan signed the National Minimum Drinking Age Act, he received a letter from a young Californian—Scott Osborne (whose mother, Kathy, was Reagan's secretary at the

White House)—writing of his goals to study architecture in college. But young Osborne could not resist adding a P.S.: "I'd just like to say one thing. If at age 18 we're old enough to vote and to fight for our country... we should be able to drink."

Reagan responded thoughtfully:

> Scott I shouldn't do this but I have to argue with you a bit on your postscript about age 18 and the right to drink.... Now don't think I'm a hypocrite, I enjoy a cocktail now and then before dinner and have a taste for a good dinner wine. I also recall feeling exactly as you do now and looking back I realize the good Lord must have been watching over me. At that age (about 18) getting drunk seemed like the thing to do, the point of drinking. Then before something too awful happened (although there were a few near scrapes) I realized that I was abusing the machinery, this body, we only get one you know. But more than that I had an example to look at. My father was an alcoholic, I loved him and I love him still but he died at age 58 and had suffered from heart disease for a number of years before his death. He was a victim of a habit he couldn't break.

And then Reagan—who was always an expert at poking fun at himself if it helped his cause—closed with:

> Forgive me for playing grandpa—but think about it a little. Become an architect or if you change your mind—whatever and we'll celebrate your graduation with a champagne toast and I'll furnish the wine.

Whether he was dealing with a Russian leader on nuclear arms control or a teenager lamenting the drinking age, Ronald Reagan—sometimes called "The Great Communicator"—was usually skilled at making his case.

TEARY-EYED TIP

"Herbert Hoover with a smile" was the way Democratic House Speaker Thomas "Tip" O'Neill Jr. sometimes referred to Ronald Reagan, but the two men also could often talk out the issues over an afternoon drink. (As his moniker implied, Tip certainly held the superior credentials when it came to hoisting a few and did his more serious imbibing with Ted Kennedy.)

The tumultuous division between parties in more recent times perhaps provides a sentimental nostalgia for one to view the O'Neill-Reagan years as more cooperative than they actually were, but, nonetheless, the term "Frenemies" does not seem too far-fetched when discussing Tip and Ronnie.

Speaking of sentiments, Reagan invited O'Neill to the White House for the speaker's sixty-ninth birthday and broke out some celebratory champagne to toast the occasion. The chief executive then burst forth with an old Irish proverb worthy of the fine wine. Lifting his glass to the Democratic warhorse, President Reagan proclaimed: "Tip, if I had a ticket to heaven and you didn't have one, I would give mine away and go to hell with you." It might have been a bit of blarney (from one Irish-American to another) but the toast brought tears to Tip O'Neill's eyes.

LAST CALL

In his Hollywood days, Reagan owned a pair of Scottish terriers that he named "Scotch" and "Soda."

When Gorbachev visited Washington in 1987, the White House staff served him American wine—but they made sure he knew the vintage was from California's Russian River region.

GEORGE H. W.

BUSH

★ 1989–1993 ★

"There is nothing more fulfilling than to
serve your country and your fellow citizens
and to do it well."

—George H. W. Bush

POPPY'S SAVVY
SOCIAL DRINKING

GEORGE HERBERT WALKER BUSH was a war hero and an outstanding baseball player—two accomplishments that most American voters admire. Bush became the youngest navy pilot in World War II, tallying nearly sixty combat missions and surviving being shot down over the Pacific. The future president was a recipient of the Distinguished Flying Cross. After the war, Bush entered Yale University, where he became a member of the Skull and Bones secret society and a team captain of the Bulldog baseball team.

By the mid-1950s, Poppy Bush was solidly established in Texas (though he later admitted that initially he hadn't really been sure what a "chicken-fried steak" might be), made money in oil, and eventually moved into politics. He won a congressional seat but lost a key Senate race to Lloyd Bentsen in 1970.

President Nixon appointed Bush to be the U.S. ambassador to the United Nations. After Nixon resigned, President Ford offered Bush the post of envoy to China in 1974. Later he served as Reagan's vice president.

Throughout his career, the elder Bush proved to be a savvy social drinker. He exhibited tolerance and—perhaps more importantly—a sense of when to stop. In short, "41"—unlike his son "43"—never had to "surrender his guns" when it came to handling alcohol.

To steal a line from an old beer commercial, Poppy knew "when to say when."

DRINKING IN CHINA

George Herbert Walker Bush kept a diary in China and later elevated it to book form (naturally called *The China Diary*). The writings document political and diplomatic happenings, but Bush also provides some interesting insights into the cultural life of his time there—including drinking and eating.

A typical example is an entry in which the future president talks about a picnic (washed down with tasty but warm beer) on the Great Wall of China:

> We climbed to the top of the left side of the wall. A real workout, tough on the legs, but exhilarating when one gets through.... It is hard to describe the spectacle of the wall.... We then drove down and had a picnic.... The sun was out. I sat in my shirt-sleeves and we ate a delicious picnic. A kind of sweet and sour fish. Excellent fried chicken. Lots of hard boiled eggs. The inevitable tasty soup. The only thing we forgot was ice so the beer was warm, but we had worked hard enough walking up to the top so that we devoured about six bottles of it. It's a heavy beer and I find it makes me sleepy but it's awful good.

When Bush returned home from his Great Wall excursion, he indulged in a hot bath and a long nap—but awoke for an 8:00 p.m. dinner consisting of caviar and a vodka martini.

Although China does not readily come to mind when beer brewing is discussed, Bush nonetheless gave it high marks in his diary:

> China goes about [brewing beer] in the same old way with excess labor and nevertheless their beer is considered very very good. We enjoy it. It seems lower in carbonation. It's more like draft beer here and it's excellent.

With the cheap Chinese prices, a typical Bush entry beams about a feast that cost less than five dollars per person:

> Peking duck dinner with a standard of 8 yuan per person. There were twelve of us—the total bill was a 119 yuan including two wines, maotai, and plenty of beer. Not bad for Peking duck.

MAOTAI MOMENTS

Needless to say, Bush (like Nixon and most other visiting Westerners) sampled some maotai—the powerful Chinese liquor of about 110 proof. He mentions this libation of hefty clout several times in his diary and, in fact, once speculates that the ultra-strong alcohol might be the cause of some disturbed sleep patterns. ("Bed at ten. Couldn't sleep at all. Maybe it's the maotai. Strong stuff.")

Sometimes maotai caused liaison Bush some political consternation, too. When the U.S. Olympic Track and Field team visited Peking in the spring of 1975, they mopped up the host squad in competition but then became a tad rowdy at a farewell banquet several days later. One can almost picture Poppy Bush wincing as he wrote:

> Return to banquet for the Chinese, give by the AAU (Amateur Athletic Union) side for the Chinese on May 29 at the International Club. Went well. [Bob] Giegengack [U.S. track coach] funny as hell. Talked as he would in an American banquet. It got out of hand, in that some of our kids got drinking too much and showing a not particularly good side. We cut off the maotai and that calmed

> That maotai really does hit a lick.

A SECRET SOCIETY SIP

George Herbert Walker Bush, a.k.a. Bush 41, a.k.a. "Poppy," came from blue-blooded northeastern stock. He naturally attended Yale University and joined the secret senior society known as Skull and Bones. Among the rumored activities of the society is "crooking," or the stealing of campus artifacts. The relics reportedly held by the society include the skulls of Martin Van Buren and Pancho Villa. In a tribute to Skull and Bones, Bush 41's cocktail is named for the secret society.

Skull and Bones Cocktail

2 muddled Maraschino cherries

2 oz. vodka

½ oz. coconut rum

1 scoop vanilla ice cream

½ cup crushed ice

Add ingredients to a blender and blend quickly just until smooth. Serve in a pint glass with a straw. Garnish with a Maraschino cherry and serve.

things down. The banquet was not unruly in an American sense, but the Chinese are so proper and so precise that I hope they were not offended by this. That maotai really does hit a lick. A great big mustached pole vaulter was the only one that really got out of hand.

COLD BEER AND NICE BUNS

Despite giving relatively high marks to Chinese beer, George H. W. Bush did not want anything to do with the native brew when it came to celebrating the Fourth of July in 1975 in Peking. In fact, he wanted the mainstays of the picnic festivities to be as American as possible. He brought in not only Miller beer, but also American cigarettes, Coca-Cola, and even American-style hot dog rolls.

At any rate, in his diary the future president proclaimed his Fourth of July celebration in China "a tremendous success." (He even tried to get John Denver "live"—but settled for blasting Denver's records.)

Bush must have been something of a "Miller Time" man back in the 1970s. Later in the summer, he visited a Chinese brewery and brought a case of Miller with him for the brewers there to sample. Bush and his party very graciously sampled the five kinds of beers the brewery was making, too.

Finding the diplomatic experience with the Chinese somewhat frustrating, Bush returned to Washington in 1976 when President Ford named him director of the Central Intelligence Agency.

QUAYLE HUNTING

There is one political theory that suggests that vice presidents make good lightning rods—meaning, they're good at drawing fire away from the president. If that is truly an asset, then James Danforth Quayle was probably a great pick as Bush's running mate in 1988.

When George H. W. Bush chose Dan Quayle, a young senator from Indiana, the supposed reasoning behind the move was that Quayle was good-looking (i.e. he might appeal to women voters) and that his politics might attract support from the conservative base of the Republican Party. (Bush was seen as somewhat moderate by some in the GOP, despite having served as Ronald Reagan's vice president for two terms.)

Today we tend to remember Quayle as the guy who instructed a schoolboy to tag an unnecessary "e" on the end of the word "potato" after the kid had spelled it correctly. But before that legacy-defining gaffe, the candidate's father James Quayle was quoted in the *New York Daily News* during the campaign as saying that his son's main interests in college had been "broads and booze."

Several days after that appeared in print, the elder Quayle attempted to backpedal, claiming that he meant to say: "If he's anything like his old man, it probably was broads and booze.... He's not like that."

All that said, quotes from former college classmates who knew Dan Quayle from his DePauw University days inevitably made references to girls, golf (Dan was a three-time letter-winner on the links), and, yes, drinking.

THE BUSHU-SURU INCIDENT

In January 1992, President George H. W. Bush paid a visit to Japan. The sixty-seven-year-old chief executive played tennis in the afternoon. Though apparently not feeling well, he still had a banquet to attend that evening—one with more than one hundred guests at the estate of Japanese prime minister Kiichi Miyazawa.

The banquet did not go exactly as planned. In fact, President Bush became suddenly nauseous and, by most accounts, promptly threw up in the lap of the Japanese prime minister, who was sitting next to him. First lady Barbara Bush rushed in with her napkin to clean up her husband (who had fainted), and Miyazawa held Bush's head in his hands. The Secret Service agents rushed to the president's side. Bush recovered quickly but was taken back to his room at Akasaka Palace and missed the rest of the evening.

Needless to say, President Bush was not available to participate in the usual rounds of toasts. But Mrs. Bush remained and participated, while National Security Advisor Brent Scowcroft proved to be an able pinch hitter when it came time for the Americans to propose a toast to their Japanese hosts. White House press secretary Marlin Fitzwater, attributing the illness to a twenty-four-hour bug, simply explained: "The President is human.... Sometimes he gets sick."

Interestingly, the incident apparently has resulted in a Japanese slang term for upchucking, or puking. Consider, say, a dozen young businessmen are out on the town in Tokyo, celebrating some major deal. One of them drinks too much and (to his embarrassment) gets physically ill. His friends might say that he demonstrated "Bushu-suru"—or "to do the Bush thing."

LAST CALL

The White House served American wines at state dinners during President George H. W. Bush's term. At a state dinner for the Australian prime minister in 1989, for example, the staff served a merlot reserve, a brut rose, and a chardonnay—all recent vintages from California, although supposedly there still was some high-priced French wines from the Nixon era down in the cellar. But as first lady Barbara Bush proudly stated: "It's our job to be selling America...."

DUBYA AND
THE THREE B'S

GEORGE W. BUSH was the second son of a president to become president. And like the first, John Quincy Adams, "W" learned about hangovers the hard way. As president, he did not have an easy first year; there was the aftermath of the "tech bubble" and, of course, the 9/11 terrorist attacks. If he did not drink during those crises, President Bush indeed deserves much credit for his steadfast resolve.

By his own admission, Bush was "a drinker" from at least his late teens to age forty. As he wrote in his autobiography: "By my mid-thirties, I was drinking routinely, with an occasional bender thrown in." He embraced what he called the "three B's"—beer, bourbon, and B&B, a sweet after-dinner digestive. But Bush experienced an epiphany after a rough night of boozing on his fortieth birthday and vowed to stop—perhaps nudged in that direction by a drumming headache and a bad case of dry mouth. Although his detractors speculated that Bush might have backslid once or twice, there is no proof that "Dubya" broke his no-alcohol pledge during his White House years. He readily gives credit to a bit of R&R—running and religion—for his successes against alcohol and smoking.

Still, Bush's drinking escapades prior to his political ascension place him firmly in the "heavyweight" category. Had the frat brothers of *Animal House* sniffed George W. Bush during his drinking heyday, they would have recognized him as one of their own.

BULLDOG WHISKEY?

Not surprisingly, some of George W. Bush's early brushes with alcohol occurred when he was a fraternity man (Delta Kappa Epsilon—DKE) at Yale. Bush's prime-time collegiate drinking moment unfolded at the prestigious Yale-Princeton football game in 1967. It is highly unlikely that any *other* future U.S. president has ever sat upon the top of a football goalpost in an inebriated state while attempting to collapse that structure. But George W. Bush did just that—and on the esteemed campus of Princeton University, no less.

By his own admission, he was a diehard Yale Bulldog. (His favorite fight song was: "Bulldog, Bulldog! Bow-Wow-Wow!") But whatever he drank at the Yale-Princeton game that fall afternoon helped the future "Decider" decide that scaling the goalpost—with gleeful intent to tear it down—was a brilliant idea. As Bush wrote in his autobiography *Decision Points*:

> ...The Princeton faithful were not amused. I was sitting atop the crossbar when a security guard pulled me down. I was then marched the length of the field and placed in a police car. Yale friends started rocking the car and shouting, "Free Bush!"

But the campus cops did not free Bush. One friend—Roy Austin, captain of the Yale soccer squad and DKE brother—jumped into the backseat of the police car to give Bush some company on the way to the station. It proved to be a good show of loyalty on Austin's part. Forty years later, President George W. Bush appointed Austin ambassador to Trinidad and Tobago.

In exchange for his freedom, the authorities insisted that the rambunctious Bulldog Bush leave Princeton and promise to never return. It seemed like a square deal, and the future president readily complied.

THE "BUSH BASH" BACKFIRE

Alcohol is never too far from the campaign trail, and Team Bush attempted to use it to attract voters during Bush's out-of-the-blue U.S. congressional bid in 1978. This political stumble occurred when an overzealous campaign volunteer placed an advertisement in the Texas Tech student newspaper that promised free beer to anyone who attended a "Bush Bash" rally.

Kent Hance—George W.'s Democratic foe—counterattacked by sending a letter concerning the "Bush Bash" (and its offer of free brew) to several thousand members of the Church of Christ, claiming that the Bush campaign tactics did not exemplify good character.

Bush lost the race, with Hance securing 53 percent of the vote. But he must have learned some lessons: Bush never lost another election.

TIE ME KANGAROO DOWN

"His first mistake was he thought he could drink with an Aussie." That was how John Newcombe, tennis titan and quaff-master from down under, later summed up the events that led to Bush's arrest on DUI charges in Kennebunkport, Maine, in 1976.

It was Labor Day weekend and "Newk"—a friend of then CIA director George H. W. Bush—was visiting the Bush family compound on Maine's picturesque coast. The affable Aussie and the younger Bush eventually felt the magnetic pull of a local watering hole and spent several hours there. Newcombe's wife Angie, Bush's sister "Doro" (a mere seventeen), and Peter Roussel (a trusted aide to Poppy Bush) were also along for the festivities.

Bush the Elder was well aware that Newcombe was not just world class on the tennis court; he also had, according to Papa Bush, a "black belt" in drinking. The son was soon to learn that this was not an exaggeration. Years later, George W. Bush would confess: "It was all a lot of fun—until the ride home."

LOOK, MOM! NO HANDS!

Since George H. W. Bush was a tennis enthusiast and an athlete of some merit, Newcombe probably shared a few tips of the trade with

> He showed me how to pick up a glass,
> with my teeth, and—without using my hands—
> chug the beer down.

his host—overhead smashes, drop shots, spin shots, and the like. Newk was certainly no less generous when it came to sharing his barroom tricks with the young George. According to Barbara Bush, this demonstration probably took place at the House-on-the-Hill—an inn less than a mile from the Bush compound at Walker's Point.

Said Bush the younger: "He [Newcombe] showed me how to pick up a glass, with my teeth, and—without using my hands—chug the beer down." When the DUI story eventually came to light years later, Bush claimed he could not remember how many beers were consumed. Newcombe put the number at a modest half dozen (presumably per participant) or so—adding with a dash of Aussie bravado: "So... not that many."

WHEN ENOUGH IS ENOUGH

"Not that many," perhaps, but enough that when Bush insisted on driving back to the compound, he swerved over the line on Ocean Drive. This did not go unnoticed by Officer Calvin Bridges, who had just gotten off his shift and was on his way home when he spied a slow-moving vehicle with two wheels over the shoulder line.

A subsequent "balloon test" soon confirmed the obvious—that the driver was over the legal limit for operating a motor vehicle in the Pine Tree State. No doubt in an effort to be helpful to all concerned, Roussel blurted out the predictable "Do you know who his father is?" to Officer Bridges. But this pronouncement failed to sway the patrolman from performing his duty.

A trip to the local police station and eventually the leveling of some modest fines followed. Bush was banned from driving in Maine for two years. Poppy Bush subjected his thirty-year-old son to the standard "take your punishment like a man" spiel. There did not appear to be any real or lasting consequences from the DUI—and Bush probably assumed there never would be.

NEVER SAY NEVER

Fast forward twenty-four years. George W. Bush is just days away from what looks to be a close presidential election against Democratic foe Al Gore. Calvin Bridges—now retired—answers the phone. It is Erin Fehlau, a reporter from Fox News. "Did you ever arrest George W. Bush for driving under the influence?"

"Ah, yup."

Bridges was quick to say that George W. Bush was "very cooperative" (notable for a guy who had been drinking beer no-hands-Newcombe-style for several hours).

Unlike George W. Bush, Calvin Bridges always suspected that one day his phone would ring concerning his strange-but-true Labor Day weekend traffic stop. If he was surprised, it probably had more to do with how long it took to happen.

Both candidate Bush and his running mate, Dick Cheney (who had two DUIs of his own), groused about the timing of the revelation—just days before the nation went to the polls. They found it difficult to believe that it wasn't some kind of "October Surprise"—a well-concealed ace—that the Dems were waiting to play at precisely the right time.

Nevertheless, the Bush-Cheney ticket prevailed in a closely contested election. How many votes it cost Bush is a matter of speculation; famed political consultant Karl Rove claims that the untimely story may have lost "W" four or five states in the 2000 election. But if one is to believe the candidate's mother Barbara, the DUI tempest definitely did cause the future president to toss and turn. "My George," bristled Barbara Bush, "could barely sleep worrying about this."

TOTALLY TRASHED

One of George W.'s less-than-stellar moments happened when he smashed his car into Poppy Bush's neighbor's trashcan in Washington, D.C., after a night out drinking over the Christmas

A DUBYA CLASSIC

While Bush 43, or "Dubya," was a teetotaler by the time he took office, he was not always this way. A fraternity member at Yale, he was nearly arrested for his drunken antics at a football game at Princeton. He later calmed down but still enjoyed his beer, bourbon, and B&B. For Dubya's drink, we're combining the beer and the bourbon in a new take on an old fashioned classic.

The Beer Old Fashioned

1 oz. lime juice
2 tsp. superfine sugar
1 oz. bourbon
3–4 oz. chilled beer (lager or pilsner)
orange peel for garnish

In an old fashioned glass, stir the lime juice, sugar, and bourbon until the sugar is dissolved. Fill the glass with ice and then add the beer. Squeeze the orange peel over the glass and drop inside.

holidays. (His sixteen-year-old brother, Marvin, was onboard for this incident.) The rubbish bin trapped beneath his vehicle apparently wasn't the only cause of subsequent sparks—George H. W. Bush demanded an explanation.

But the intoxicated Dubya was far from apologetic and—according to many reports—challenged his father to go *mano a mano* to settle the issue. Younger brother Jeb reportedly stepped in (and by some accounts, Barbara Bush, too) with the timely news that George had recently received word of his acceptance at the Harvard Business School—and the situation was defused. As for the father-son confrontation, it was merely an alcohol-fueled blip on the screen, as, these days, George W. unfailingly refers to "41" with great affection and admiration.

THE EPIPHANY

Twenty years after he'd scaled the goalpost at Princeton and ten years after the Labor Day weekend screw-up in Kennebunkport, George W. Bush said: "No mas." In writer Pete Hamill's memoir *A Drinking Life* on why he had quit, Hamill finally concluded that he just didn't have the talent for it. Bush presumably came to a similar conclusion, and, in his case, it would have been a difficult one to argue against.

Bush's revelation happened the day after his fortieth birthday. He had been celebrating enthusiastically with some close friends at the beautiful Broadmoor resort in Colorado Springs. Since Colorado Springs is at relatively high altitude, it is somewhat easier to reach a state of intoxication than at sea level. Mr. Bush apparently ignored this peril (or, like drinking head-to-head with Newcombe, wrongly assumed that any red-blooded Texan was up to the challenge) and overindulged. Silver Oak wine at sixty dollars

> Bush remembers the bar tab as "colossal."

per bottle was the libation of choice, and Bush remembers the bar tab as "colossal."

So was the headache. The next day, Mr. Bush attempted to go for a run—his go-to activity when it came to counterattacking a morning hangover. He could barely shuffle along. The future leader of the free world suddenly arrived at a moment of clarity— if he was to honor his family, reach his potential, and serve God, then Demon Alcohol needed to be banished:

> Faith showed me a way out. I knew I could count on the grace of God to help me change. It would not be easy, but by the end of the run, I had made up my mind; I was done drinking.

RUNNING FROM THE DEVIL

George W. Bush credits running with an assist in his ability to quit both drinking and smoking. He first started running (on a dare from a friend) in 1972, when, as he puts it, "I was a man who was known to drink a beer or two." Bush actually became a semi-competitive runner with a 5K time of sub-twenty minutes. As Bush related to *Runner's World* editor Bob "Wish" Wischnia in a 2002 interview:

> As a runner, I quickly realized what it felt like to be healthy, and I already knew what it felt like to be unhealthy. If you're drinking too much, and you're running to cure a hangover, pretty soon you have to make a choice. Do you want to keep getting a hang-over, or do you want to feel the way you do after a run? Running is a way to heal people. Running is something that just makes you feel fantastic.

BAD KARMA

Back when George Bush was drinking with some dedication, he once blurted out at a Kennebunkport dinner party hosted by his parents to an older (but attractive) woman: "So... How is sex after fifty?" This comment resulted in a suffocating silence around the dinner table.

To his credit, Bush later apologized. But the incident was not completely forgotten. When Bush (then the governor of Texas) turned fifty, a note arrived at the Governor's Mansion. It was supposedly from the offended female guest from his parents' dinner party from years before. "Well, George," read the message, "how is it?"

Whoever she was, she had a good sense of humor.

LAST CALL

As a brazen adolescent, George once poured vodka in the fishbowl and thereby terminated his little sister Doro's pet goldfish.

Appearing at a state dinner with the Queen of England, President George W. Bush noticed there were seven wine goblets at his place setting. "Apparently the Royal Pantry had not gotten the word that I no longer drank," Bush later joked.

LIST OF COCKTAILS